Pushing Treacle Uphill

by

John Featherstone

Grosvenor House
Publishing Limited

The right of John Featherstone to be identified as the author of this
work has been asserted in accordance with Section 78
of the Copyright, Designs and Patents Act 1988

The book cover picture is copyright to John Featherstone

This book is published by
Grosvenor House Publishing Ltd
28-30 High Street, Guildford, Surrey, GU1 3EL.
www.grosvenorhousepublishing.co.uk

A CIP record for this book
is available from the British Library

ISBN 978-1-78148-994-9

FOR
SHIRLEY

Contents

	Page
Foreword	ix
Chapter One	1
Chapter Two	17
Chapter Three	28
Chapter Four	34
Chapter Five	49
Chapter Six	65
Chapter Seven	75
Chapter Eight	83
Chapter Nine	91
Chapter Ten	99
Chapter Eleven	107
Chapter Twelve	133
Chapter Thirteen	141
Chapter Fourteen	149
Chapter Fifteen	157

With a special thanks to

RITA HARROD
CPR

For her much valued advice and
encouragement at every step of my story.

Foreword

I should have written this account of my life years ago. In my seventies now, but that bit better qualified perhaps to tell a story. No surprise to those that know me that I have opinions and reflections and plenty to say at times, but I do listen as well. It has been written for my own satisfaction, but with I hope, pathos and humour in equal measure.

I have no wish to displease or offend anyone who reads it. I also say sorry for some mistakes I made over the years. I do not need to use any swear words for effect, or seek other than to speak from the heart. It's just a telling of life experience for those who know me and for a memory of my ever loving sister Shirley, because I should have written this a year ago for her to read before it was too late. If others choose to read it – then thank you. It will be for them to enjoy or otherwise. I hope it is the former, but I make no apology for telling it other than the way life was meant to be.

I did some aimless wandering but I did meet Howard Hughes, was backstage with the Beatles, was a Police motorcyclist traffic officer, worked with Barry Sheene of

Suzuki and walked across Britain. This in between attempting to drink my way out of problems, and also be a Dad to my two children. Most of all I found the love of my life in the last forty years...

'In the end we will remember not the words of our enemies, but the silence of our friends.'
-Edmund Burke, Irish 18th century politician.

Saying that, I have some wonderful memories of friendship, love and help from many friends and family. I try to retain the same humour and wry reflective look at life and always have the ability to stand up and be counted. Enjoy reading it and find something that makes you think...

'Well, he would say that wouldn't he'
-John Featherstone (2016)

Chapter One

I had never seen Mum cry before.

Blackpool, Lancashire in 1950 and I was seven years old and been told to wait outside a grey faceless building on the North Promenade near to Cocker Square. She came out crying and reached for me and I pressed against her, not knowing what to say or do. 'Come on' she said. 'Let's go for a walk down the front to make us better.' I must have asked what was wrong and she said, 'they can't help us at the moment to live anywhere else, but we'll get by so don't you worry. Mum will always look after you.' The smile and the warm hand of Josie was back to guide me onwards, as it did for all the years to come.

Welcome to post war Blackpool and the Golden Mile. The land of opportunity and the visit to the National Assistance Board to be told that we did not qualify for any housing help or benefits of any kind. My dad Tom Featherstone had died the year before aged 48, when we lived in Tutbury near Burton on Trent, Staffordshire, with sister Shirley who was seven years older than me. Twenty years in the card room of the

Mutual Cotton mill in Heywood, Lancashire our home town had taken its toll on Dad and decimated his health as conditions did with thousands of others. Death due to bronchial pneumonia it said on the death certificate -he had managed to transfer to a clerical job at MU 43 an RAF Maintenance unit at Pilsworth, Heywood in 1939 as the war years loomed and then, after I was born, was transferred to Tutbury to another MU depot.

I was born at 7, Prospect Place, Heywood on the 14th June 1943. Shirley with her soon developed sense of humour always called me the golden boy, supposedly something to do with the mass of fair curls that I still look at on an early photograph. Just a few grey strands now, but the name stuck for many years if sibling rivalry arose, but her devotion and love for me was never in doubt – and I miss her. Within one year Dad was transferred to Tutbury and the green swards of Staffordshire were around us.

My first memories of Green Lane, Tutbury in the upstairs maisonette that went with his job, are with me today-but I could only have been five or six years old. We lived on the outskirts of the village with cows grazing in the fields bordering the houses on Green Lane. I had the idea to remove stair rods (the wooden triangular ones some two foot long) from the stair carpet to provide rounding up sticks when Mum was busy in the kitchen. Essential for my new friends to venture over the back fence and attempt to herd the reluctant moo cows. The more vivid memory a few months later in 1949, of kneeling on a chair to see out of the front upstairs window looking at Mum being driven off in a car. A split second scene that has lived in

my mind for ever. Turned out that Dad had been transferred back to the RAF Pilsworth MU offices a few
weeks earlier and his resultant death in hospital that
night determined our family future. Within weeks Mum
and Shirley, with me in tow, had to leave the tied house
where happiness was the norm and decision taken to go
to Blackpool to be near Auntie Ivy and family… and
find somewhere to live. No money but the prospects of
work at least existed in the holiday town where I was to
grow up in my teens. Refuge was the front room of a
council house on Powell Avenue with the Bell's. A large
easy going family who were happy to increase the
family of seven to make it ten, for a bit of extra rent
money. All very on the QT as it was referred to. My
initial stay was brief as Mum took on cleaning jobs,
selling rock on a seafront stall and café work to try and
keep us together. It could not last in the cramped conditions and shared bedrooms and living space so no room
at the inn I suppose and the painful decision that Mum
had to take, to let me go and live with my maternal
grandmother back in Heywood.

That lasted for some two special and memorable
years for me as, not for the first time, I was protected
from the harsh reality of growing up. My wonderful
Nan who, from poor Irish origins had a life that was
typical of the times. A sturdy independent lady who
always dressed in black and lived alone now at 134,
Pilsworth Road, Heywood in a small two up and down
with outside toilet. As most did in Cotton Town! Six
children, two who died in the war and a husband
long gone, who it is said turned up at the family
home in Bamford Road between drinking bouts and
prison stays, to keep the population going. She in the

meantime would somehow sort all her children out for school and then trek across the fields for a mile or two to the mill for the daily shift. Yes, that was a daily routine for many. I did not know it but as I write this now, not for the first time, I am reminded how inspirational she was for me. Unstinting love and fierce maternal protection. A no nonsense type who would be in her sixties when I went to live with her at seven years old and was enrolled at the local Bullough Moor Primary School just down Pilsworth Road.

A fantastic story teller of tales designed to fit the moment – nearly always told in front of the black leaded grate where we spent every evening in summer and winter. The one about the little boy who was caught writing a swear word on a railing …he was sent to an approved school by the police and had to wash every morning outside in a bathtub of cold water and always made to keep clean. Was taught to be kind to girls especially those like my sister Shirley, who I should always look after and have good manners and especially other mothers and help them off the bus and so on. All magically told to suit any guidance and growing up situation. Some might have had a goldfish in a bowl. We had a striped perch complete with the prickly back spine, caught in a local mill pond that amazingly lived for over two years in his watery confines in the tiny front room. A simple life filled with guidance and love.

The coal shed was the outhouse lean to and I was carefully positioned in the kitchen to watch and count the empty bags as they were thrown onto the floor in the small yard at delivery times. My first spying mission in life, but treated with utmost importance. Money was never mentioned other than we did not have any or not much, but it was not important. The treat was being sent to the Chippy down the road perhaps twice a week. Fish 8 pence and chips 4 pence and don't forget to ask for crispy bits she said. 'You haven't brought any back - did you ask properly?' was the challenge when she unwrapped them from the newspaper on my return.

A sometimes crowded shop and I was probably at that early age too embarrassed to speak up and ask. She worked out my shyness after a few times, when I returned without the crispy bits of batter, so on one of her rare trips out down the road to the cobblers to have new irons put on her clogs (still wearing them from her working days in the mill), the matter was resolved. She called in the chip shop herself and saw the owners. 'That grandson of mine can't bring himself to speak up and ask for bits. Can you remember when he comes in' Job done and I doubt they would have thought to argue with her anyway.

The ultimate treat was the weekly trip by train on a Saturday to Bury Market some three miles away from Broadfield rail station just up from her house. We also had a dodgy clock on the mantelpiece that was always losing time, so I was told to stand at the front door and ask anyone passing the right time. No problem at dinnertime on most Saturdays when the local men went to support Bury football club at Gigg Lane and caught the train from Broadfield. Bury is still the home of the black pudding where we would sit on a form by the gardens near the market stalls and like many others, eat the staple food of the north out of wrapped paper with a fork you brought yourself from home. Imagine an eight year old today doing that-got to say I passed on the mustard that was obligatory for adults. Or even the larger than usual pieces of fat in the pudding that I gave to Nan. But it was proper food that was part of my growing up and now years later a reinvented delicacy featured on a top restaurant menu.

A date I always remember was February 6th 1952 when King George 6th died. I was in Mr Corcoran's class at school that morning and the Headmaster Mr Johnson came in to say 'You are all going home early because the King has died.' Which of course meant an extra playing out day with friends Trevor Proctor, Jim Freeman, Roy Greeves and Rod Warburton, who all lived nearby. Part of the newly formed Station Field gang next to Spencer's Farm which was across the road from the terraced houses where we lived. The cobbled road leading up to the sidings of Broadfield Rail station and the waste land surrounding the farm was ours. It was February, but we all had little memory of the seasons and rain and snow did not stop play. Soggy black pumps or shoes with holes in the sole, but no matter. Never even noticed or cared. Suppose we were governed by day and night only -darkness meant you had to be indoors.

Throwing arrows were the must have accessory where a loop of string propelled a thin cane with weighted and sharpened end and cardboard flights to ideally replicate a javelin. It was an acceptable weapon, other than a catapult that carried the possibility of confiscation. What we really wanted was a machete that was amazingly advertised in the Exchange and Mart as a mail order item for several shillings? – might as well have said a thousand pounds. Was probably listed along with gardening items for hacking down the undergrowth in the gardens of a stately home, but we would have seen it differently. I have no memory of wet or dry clothes or even having many at all. Or indeed the mile walk to school in all weathers and back on my own, crossing roads with little traffic and a small park area, with a dilapidated bandstand to reach the school yard. But I was told repeatedly never to speak to strange men and not to dawdle.

I do recall the amazing frost patterns in winter on the inside of the windows in all but the front room that had the open fire. The upstairs bed shared with Nan for warmth in those early years and the bedroom with fire grate never lit even on the coldest days. But then I don't remember ever being ill or off school during the two years. We did though have much looked forward to visits. Auntie Ivy who was a few years younger than Mum, was standing the markets around Lancashire and with husband Fred used to go to Bury on a Monday and call to see us on the way back home to Blackpool most weeks and bring pies and cakes (that was the bit that mattered). Coming home from school I used to look out for the green van parked outside and the treats that followed. I was always encouraged to write a few lines to Mum and Shirley back in Blackpool and she would take them with her or we would post them on at times. These faded pages she kept are with me to this day and I smile at the words I used and the rather stark delivery. Here is an example of what a young mind was thinking.

'Dear Mother, I am OK. My Nan is OK. The fish is still living. We received the fifteen shillings. I and Nan received the money off Auntie Ivy. We thank Shirley for the picture card. I hope you are OK. I have made something for you (mother). Will you ask Auntie Ivy if she saw the ration book because we can't find them, love from Nan John xx'And another short letter with a little more feeling.

'Dear Mother and Shirley, I hope you are OK. I went up Pilsworth with Trevor, David and Roy Greeves on Saturday to Stony Dell. We were up there three hours. I got some flowers for Nan called Marsh Marigolds, comfrey and some gipsy grass. I am just finishing my letter to give Auntie Ivy. Love from John and Nan xxx'

I had my first brush with the rights and wrongs of life on a visit to see Uncle Les, Auntie Nell and cousin Pat (some three years younger) who lived at 1, Ormerod Street nearer the town centre. Mum had come over on a visit and we went for tea to their house. In a small crowded front room I was sitting near the sideboard, when I saw a sixpence piece placed near to a vase of flowers and hidden from view. I decided perhaps it had been forgotten, or more likely did not think at all and carefully slid it into my trouser pocket as all the adults were talking. The afternoon passed and we were ready to walk back home to Pilsworth Road when an arm went round my shoulders from Uncle Les who said quietly. 'I think you should put it back, because it's not yours.' I would have mumbled something about 'thinking it was nobody's' and filled up with shame and probably had a burning red face. I reached into my pocket and gave it to him and he said 'It was left by another Auntie for your cousin Pat on her birthday. Just remember and think on in future' A stare at me and a squeeze on the shoulder and I was quietly sent on my way.... nothing more was said. No charges brought, but a valuable lesson in life.

The 1950's arrive and a return to Blackpool for me and living back with Mum who, true to form was always trying to better herself and do her best for us. Not that I gather it pleased Nan too much who was sorry to see me go and led to a difficult time for her being once again on her own. She died in 1957 at age 73. I went to Hawes Side Lane junior school for the last year before passing my eleven plus exam and entry to Blackpool Grammar School.

I have several happy enough memories of Hawes Side but one in particular when the lady teacher whose name I forget asked us to do an essay-the word was probably composition, but she suggested it should be an exciting story and left it to our imagination. By this time I was an avid reader of the weekly comics Adventure, Rover, Hotspur and Wizard. Not that I could afford to buy them, but they always became available as borrows or trades. I had read Treasure Island, Robinson Crusoe and any other adventure books I could find. So the plot soon hatched that to copy, with a small alteration, a pirate tale from one of the comics would do the trick as nobody else would know. I filled the required four pages of the exercise book and handed it in.

The next day all were given back except mine... I probably shuffled with some sort of dread but then the words from teacher. 'I have kept this one back to read out to you written by John Featherstone. It is absolutely wonderful' or something like that was said. Eyes swivelled towards me from classmates who were seeing a genius in their midst, or at least knew me enough not to be convinced. I somehow kept a head down mumbling of 'Thank you Miss' and the torture was soon over when it was read out. One puzzled lad in class did say afterwards. 'I know about them capturing that pirate ship The Jolly Roger on the Spanish Main and what happened because I've read it somewhere' Some years later I was acquainted with the word plagiarism, but at the time it was the brainwave that nobody else would have thought of. So at least I was doing some lateral thinking or creating opportunist ploys that would serve me well over the next few years on Blackpool's Golden Mile.

The word deception I would not have understood. Home in Blackpool was still in different live in situations where ideally a room went with the job Mum managed to get and two young children were accepted. Not easy. All the time it was the checking and asking by Mum to see if her name was still on a council list. At last the much longed for two bedroom house was given to us on Dingle Avenue, Grange Park when I was around 14 years old. Two years before that and things became more settled due to Mum meeting a gentle man in every respect in Jack Sagar, who came into our three lives and who was to become my stepdad a few years later when they married. We had made our home with him when he bought a house on Winton Avenue in Marton having lived with his mother back in Preston after his divorce. He had two sons and worked as a welder at Leyland Motors.

A lifelong ballroom dancing interest led him to weekly visits to the famous Tower Ballroom where Mum went from time to time with lady friends she had met. That was the social scene, certainly not pubs and before long we were introduced to him and he helped make all the things happen for me, whilst not being able to do the same with his own sons. I paid a tribute to him in a story I entitled 'Funny Turns' which was one of my early pieces from a creative writing course I went to later in the 1990's with the countryman Jack Benson of the local Evening Gazette. Certainly more to say about him as the chapters continue.

Stories of coincidence that unfold not just in my life I suspect...a recurring theme and perhaps a chance meeting or opportunity that determines your destiny in life. Very strange as though on reflection it was all that life is meant to be. The quick decision that reaps a reward and satisfaction, or leads to a time of sadness and despair. The Golden Mile years arrive for me as the 1950's progress and Blackpool Grammar School and the final year for Shirley at Collegiate High School for Girls leaving with some five GCSE's and lifelong friends. I became a fag. Which was the dated name for the first year intake of eleven year olds at Raikes Parade Grammar School on Church Street, some half mile from Blackpool seafront in 1954. My form master's Mr Jones and then Mr Rigby wearing the obligatory BSC or MA academic gowns from qualifying probably at Oxford or Cambridge for a degree. The headmaster was the Very Reverend H M Luft who was still able to dispense strokes of the cane for the more serious misdemeanours.

This was all accepted at the time probably with pride from parents that their young son was going to the grammar school rather than a secondary modern, but looking back it was clearly a hangover from Empire days when the public school structure created supposedly educated real men who were going to rule the country, if not the world. The word 'fag' was the lowest form of life whose mission was to be the servant of prefects and masters. Long gone by then in public schools even but the tales and pretence lived on to establish that you knew your place. Some minor form of bullying became the norm till the second years schooling arrived and a new set of fodder arrived to be treated with disrespect. Strange early years with an onslaught of forgettable French, Latin Chemistry and religious instruction. Algebra and Geometry lessons from Mr Cowley, that must have taken place as I stared out of the window failing to understand. We must have had some attempt at wood work lessons, but five years after walking into the school I probably could not knock a nail in straight or even wire up a 3 pin plug.

My reading and interest though in History and Geography came to the fore and I was mostly top placed in any exams-but only in those two subjects. Teachers that you stood up for as they entered the classroom and always call Sir. The character ones that inevitably had nicknames such as the French teacher Mr 'Drip' Murdoch who was probably in the early stages of Alzheimer's or some other mind sapping disturbance that coping with young boys did not help. When I saw the various films of 'Goodbye Mr Chips' in later years, I regret I was part of those thoughtless times the way we schoolboys treated him. A kindly talented man, who was just pushing treacle uphill with us lot. A dated academic system that should have been buried when the war ended-the First World War that is.

But out of it came the friendships with some I retain to this day. Dave Miller. A talented drummer who made us all sit up when at 12 years old he appeared on television in a talent show called 'All your Own' presented by Huw Wheldon later to be a top name at the BBC. Dave's father played the drums at local clubs and and encouraged him from an early age. He went on to be the drummer with Jimmy Justice, Marty Wilde and the Wildcats and Joe Brown and the Bruvvers in the vibrant sixties. Friends at school made in that first year included Robert Simpson, John Gledhill, Bill Taylor, Barrie Oughton and others departed such as Phil Crossley. All of us sharing the same enthusiasm for motorbikes in early teens to follow on from the cow horn handlebars that had transformed the staid bicycles we used for transport. A child being dropped off at school in a car? – certainly not. It was bus, bicycle and shank's pony.

Bill Haley and his Comets and the Blackboard Jungle film were signs of the new awakening for us teenagers. Just what lusty young minds wanted as the existence of girls became a topic of conversation and the world out there was changing fast. The days when you stood around at the cinema kiosk looking at the magic words X Certificate film. You asked someone to take to you to see a horror film such as X the Unknown. Can you believe that – but it happened and then the strange man you asked wanted to sit next to you. The great awakening that girls had an attraction as their and our bodies 'changed' as it was carefully referred to. The Collegiate school was some 500 yards to the east near Stanley Park on Beech avenue. A road to be crossed at peril from in house school rules, that viewed the courting of the opposite sex with disapproval. Homosexuality was probably alive and well, but always swept under the carpet and would never have been mentioned other than a reference to 'I think he's a queer' not really understanding what one was. The word lesbian never mentioned or would have been understood.

Prejudice was something that was an opinion passed as fact. It was easy to be labelled that if you did not have a girlfriend by your late teens for instance that something was wrong with you. Applied to lots of other abrupt and dismissive attitudes. The thoughtless comments made to me in the first year at grammar when I got free school dinner tickets because of Mum being a widow. 'Is your Dad dead then? Is that why you get them and the free bus tickets?' I had learnt in those last two years to remain silent, but always squirmed a little and did not want to talk as the pain was still there knowing how my background was so different from many others at the school. The other kids whose parents had a boarding house or perhaps a business in the town.

Mum had been sent a letter saying I was entitled to free clothing from the Chief Constable's Clothing Fund. It was in the old Police Station buildings of South King Street, with its own entrance on Charnley Road. I was told to go there and see what was available and true to form I dodged the 'have you been there yet' after saying it was closed the first time. I then confessed that I would do without because someone might see me going in. Understanding as always reaction from Mum and nothing more said.

Despite the downsides the structure and school rules created a sense of unity and probably pride at being at the Grammar that seemed to come to most of us. No better than when at special assemblies in the school hall it was announced that we would finish with the school song. For us it was a rousing number called Tarantara. Only later was it revealed, for those paying attention that the song title was 'When the Foeman Bares his

Steel' the wonderful chorus song from Gilbert and Sullivan's 'Pirates of Penzance'. The deep bass of English teacher Bill Breeze who would be in his early sixties probably, on stage with piano accompaniment by music teacher Leslie Whittaker.

The same Bill Breeze who swept into class and anyone who had the stupidity not to stand up when he entered had the possibility of the slipper across the backside. He always carried it inside his gown and sometimes during a lesson if he perhaps thought attention was slipping he would place it on top of the desk with nothing said. Early mind games? In any corridor the sound of the crash of chairs and swift movement was enough to show that it was his class being taken. It worked though and the threat was enough. But back to the school song.

I can recall the libretto today from memory, even if my voice did not match my enthusiasm. The chorus accompaniment from the wives and girlfriends (in our case the first and second year pupils with unbroken voices) was really something and always sung at top pitch with enthusiasm... The ultimate was the annual speech and prize day at the Palace Theatre on the Promenade next to the Tower, when this was sung by the whole school of some 500 pupils and the masters.

When the foeman bares his steel. Tarantara, tarantara.
We uncomfortable feel. Tarantara.
And we find the wisest thing. Tarantara, tarantara.
Is to slap our chests and sing. Tarantara.
For when threatened with emeutes. Tarantara, tarantara.
And your heart is in your boots. Tarantara.

There is nothing brings it round like the trumpet's martial sound, like the trumpet's martial sound.

Tarantara, tarantara, tarantara... And then the chorus comes in...

'Go ye heroes go to glory, though ye die in combat gory *Ye shall live in song and story go to immortality. Go to death and go to slaughter-die and every Cornish daughter, with her tears your grave shall water. Go ye heroes go and die. Tarantara, tarantara, tarantara'*

Chapter Two

Stirring stuff and it did create something in us I'm sure of pride and achieving. Life had become more settled for Mum though she always still took part time shop work. Shirley was now engaged to Ron Milburn who she had met at Dean Street Holy Trinity Youth Club in South Shore. Marriage soon followed at the church there. I have been looked after protected and encouraged and hopefully taught to give before taking always with good manners The freedom and employment years are here. With it again being Blackpool, the opportunity to earn and achieve perhaps easier than it would have been in an inland industrial town. The sheer explosion of visitor numbers, many who were going on holiday for the first time in their lives after the war years.

It was Harold Macmillan who famously said in 1957 that some of us had never had it so good and it turned out to be very true. Of course he was right, but my teenage mind would not have thought about doing other than living for the moment and hopefully going where life took me. I was not planning any saving schemes or property investments or regretting not trying harder at school to obtain GCE qualifications.

At the same time in mid to late teens was not sure what I wanted to do-I was reasonably happy I suppose doing a driving job and delivering groceries to hotels along the promenade followed by the move to Leonard Heys and various goods to the shops from Fleetwood to Lytham St Anne's and Kirkham. Apart from a lot of TV and electrical goods, they had a cycle and motorcycle parts division that helped to introduce me to the world of two wheels. I also had a new best friend called Buster. A cross collie dog who came to us from Colne in east Lancashire. A wonderful temperament and my companion in the cab of the delivery vans. He never needed to be on a lead. Typical of the fantastic breed, he responded to looks and a silent understanding and would sit in the driver's seat in the open doored cab as my personal security officer, or walk along beside me across busy roads. I had my first moment of printed fame with him that warranted a short story write up in the local Evening Gazette. It was entitled 'Driver takes his own Fire to the Fire Station in Fleetwood'.

I had finished my early morning delivery round to TV and electrical and cycle shops in Thornton Cleveleys and Fleetwood in my Bedford van that had large sliding doors for entry and exit. The door rails recess at the side of the cab often accumulated empty fag packets, fish and chip paper and betting slips ... I remember coming up the busy main Lord Street from the pier when smoke started to fill the cab, as my best friend barked with alarm next to me. Soon sussed out that yet another discarded cigarette had not flicked properly through the side window and had found an ability to become an incendiary device I slid the door back and forth-still driving at some twenty mile an hour as you do. Exactly what not to do, if I had thought for a moment longer. Smoke now swirling out of window and even pedestrians waving to me.

Quick thinking needed and a swerve to the right across the tram tracks and onto Radcliffe road near to RR Thomas Cycle repair shop and my new destination-the Fleetwood Fire Brigade HQ. Smartly out of the cab with Buster, who did not hang around and jumped out with me. I told him to wait on guard near the van as the distinctive smell of burning paper swirled up through the now fully open door. I ran across the forecourt and tapped on the glass. The desk officer looked up and I said something like. 'Got a bit of a problem – van's on fire, have you got something to put it out?' A real comedy routine I suppose, but I did not see it that way as he hit the RED button and a siren sounded and I got a full turn out of the brigade right in front of the station. Amazingly no damage caused after a hosing down of the cab area and another lesson of life. A suggestion from the Station Officer that 'perhaps smoking while driving and only hopefully tossing fag ends out of windows was not a good idea'. True to form the Gazette sniffed out the story as I did my best to drive back to Blackpool and keep quiet about it. Buster was back in the passenger seat and he was not going to grass me up. Home to Dingle Avenue first to gather my wits and the usual dinner of a tin of Crosse & Blackwell's tomato soup, barm cake and a bag of chips. The obligatory transistor radio switched on in the kitchen and Workers Playtime from some factory with happy employee's who were only setting the place alight with songs.

Talking of fires. A large woodworks at Crossley's Bridge on Bispham Road in Blackpool sold joinery off cuts on Saturday mornings in the earlier years and if you had the much desired set of old pram wheels to convert then a load could be bought filling your own sacks at the depot yard, taken home, cut up and tied into smaller bundles for selling to the neighbours. The real prize of having a set of pram wheels or similar was the Bagging you could do from North and Central Rail stations when the excursion trains arrived at weekends with Wakes weeks holiday makers and families. The approach always the same. 'Can I carry your bags Mister?' The next question was vital if they accepted. 'Have you been to Blackpool before' The hoped for answer was No. In that case, if the boarding house was nearby on Albert Road or Adelaide Street, then perhaps a slight detour round other streets and alleys was in order to increase the fee and hoped for tip.

This ploy helped to supplement the days roaming with mates on the Pleasure Beach. Always eyes checking the ground to spot a coin and when the machine attendants not around, a careful wedge of paper up the Win slot on the flick ball machines. This to retain any reward after disgruntled winning punter had smacked the glass front a couple of times without success and walked off in disgust. We never saw it as other than enterprising and a laugh, but it was not something to be proud of. The independence was given and in the main I was allowed to decide what I did from the early caring upbringing. Not that I would have rushed to disclose any Pleasure Beach amusement scams.

Early well intended attempts with after class advice at school, to suggest you should plan your career future and think what you wanted to achieve in life… What do you want to do when you leave school? Not a clue other than work which was taken for granted, earn lots of money, play the guitar and become a rock and roll star. Will that do? Not that I was ever brave enough to say anything like that.

Most of all I really was in the land of opportunity in Blackpool and not grey cotton town inland Lancashire as the economy fired up and the visitors from the northern working towns arrived like sheep to the slaughter. The Wakes weeks of summer meant that they had money to spend and spend – it's now known as disposable income. Myself and others with growing awareness had a mission in life… To help them do just that and with already established money raising schemes we did. There was also the bonus of fishing off the North and Central Pier Jetties and something that Dave Miller, Rob Simpson and I became good at. Common to see hundreds lining the jetty rails with greenheart wood rods and the new multiplier reels that you cast out some distance being careful to keep to cast very straight, to avoid the mouthful of abuse of those next to you. Fresh air, freezing fingers and face and the smell of the sea. Small flatfish known as dabs in spring and autumn, codling and whiting in winter and night lining as tides rose in the cold months. A line with spaced hooks at low tide up to 100 yards long, weighted in the sand at each end, and baited up with blackworm and lugworm. Wait till the tide covered it then back to retrieve some eight hours later, as the incoming high tide then receded. This would mean going in freezing pre dawn's at times, but the rewards worth it, but only when the westerly winds came in off the Irish Sea. No trouble getting out of bed if the valuable night line you shared with mates had good pickings of up to 4lb codling. Ideal was when a moderate west wind blew as the fish do not usually feed on easterly winds off the land. The sea then is clearer and flat and the sand undisturbed by wave action. Local knowledge and tips of where and when, passed down by the pier fishermen of the Fylde Coast and there were a lot of them. All ages and prepared to brave the cold and lashing waves that swept over the jetty as high tide approached. The dreaded "everyone off" called down by the pier attendant as the waves chopped through the metal slats of the jetty with a terrifying roar just as the fish started biting in earnest. Health and Safety? More like near mass drowning being imminent – not that we did other than complain bitterly and certainly never saw the danger.

I had my first proper job at 13 as a paper boy delivering the Blackpool Evening Gazette and doing a morning round as well. The 12/6p a week was very welcome from Roberts Newsagents on Newhouse Road, Marton where nearly every home in the area had it delivered. Seven am in the morning start with plenty of Mirrors, Daily Herald and Express. My round was Newhouse Road along to James Avenue and along Penrose and the streets between including Elaine, June and Winton Avenues to end back at the shop with an empty bag and get ready for the 3 or 3a bus along Newhouse and Park roads to school before 9am. Deliveries again with the Gazette to probably the same houses at 5 pm. The best of all being the week before Christmas when the once a year knock on the door was expected with the standard greeting 'Compliments of the season from your paper boy'

'Oh right – hang on a minute lad and I'll get my purse' or the shout to him inside who came and gave anything from one shilling, half a crown was good or the memorable one from clearly imbibed building site working in all his muck and just in from work with cheery smile saying. 'Here you are sunshine-you deserve it". A ten shilling note!'

The paper round finished when we moved to the council house on the fairly new estate of Grange Park when I would be 14 or 15 and that summer would bring my full time job at weekend's and school holidays with Naventi's ice cream. With it came a few settled years in my life when the small garden at Dingle Avenue took my interest for vegetable growing. Even a few rows of potatoes in the front garden which did well and caused amusement to the neighbours. The early post school years with plenty of friends and outside interest in life and some interest in girls but nothing more than that.

The first steady van driving job with J T Youd Wholesale Grocers and then followed the same at an electrical and cycle/ motorcycle wholesalers Leonard Heys who were based on Field Street next to the Blackpool Football Club on Bloomfield Road. No doubt this motorcycle association helped later in life and even while still at school, the first trip to the Isle of Man in June to see the TT Races.

Excitement started with the midnight sailing of the Isle of Man Steam Packet Company ferry from Fleetwood to Douglas. Passenger ships that sailed to the Isle of Man for years such as the 'Ben my Chree' 'Tynwald' 'Mona's Queen' and the latest being the 'Manxman' Then the dawn trek up the Snaefell mountain to be roadside and see the likes of Mike Hailwood and Giacomo Agostini hurtle past at over a hundred miles an hour on exotic Italian MV Agusta machines within yards, as we sat on the banking above Creg ny Baa. The evocative smell of burning Castrol R race oil and the excitement of speed as they continued down the Hillberry straight on the route to the start finish line in Douglas. The exciting stuff of boy's dreams that came true. I was there at the premier road race circuit in the whole world when Bob McIntyre was the first to lap the 37 ¾ mile circuit at over 100 miles an hour. Motorcycles that were to become a large part of my working life with Suzuki GB and Italian companies such as Piaggio Vespa and Aprilia, but at the same I know sadness for many who have family and friends seriously injured, or who lost their lives with this mode of transport.

Phil Crossley and I went on a Friday day trip one June (not sure how we got off school) as before on the midnight ferry from Fleetwood to see the Senior 500cc race. The start had been delayed due to rain and a further delay, then finally announced on the loud-speakers round the course, that it was cancelled till the following day due to mist on Snaefell mountain behind us. Realisation came slowly-we should have been back at the boat terminal. We had the prospect then of walking back to the docks in Douglas with wet feet, cold and hungry and with only a return boat ticket in our pockets, but we did have the sight of our Fleetwood bound ship sailing majestically out of the harbour on a grey afternoon as we looked down on Douglas harbour. The night was spent huddled in a promenade shelter with several other Lancashire bound bodies who were shipped back the next morning. All part of growing up

Going back to the summer jobs though-Shirley and her friends at school had already trodden this work path selling ice creams on the sands, so natural enough for me to follow and contribute to the family income. The total hours a week working all seven days of course were simple and decided by when the tide was in or out and if the sun was shining. Long days for the same wage around three pounds a week I think and if it rained and was set in for the day, you got sent home early after washing ice cream containers, other odd jobs and best of all taking cars in for parking at the garage that also stored the ice cream trailers. No contract of employment. Cash in hand-take it or leave it. We took for granted the ability soon developed to play with 'big boys toys' as they might be known today. Some of the fifteen foot single axle ice cream trailers were stored in the car garage as well, so hitching them up to the Land Rover and reversing them into a narrow gap also became an art form as you have to apply opposite lock and fine judgement. The confidence of youth though and no problem. Kenny Robinson who worked there as well and lived just off Talbot Road, was my doubles partner in the art of car and trailer parking...and was probably a bit ahead of me at the time in street wise credibility, but I soon caught up. 'You have to leave your keys Mister and we will park it over there for you.' Potential customer would perhaps say: 'Hang on a minute – will it get moved or bumped and still be locked up.' Confident reply 'Oh of course. Very safe, because we have to have the keys just in case of emergency and probably won't need to move it' That was the key word 'probably' as more than likely the car would be moved-the mileage would probably not have been checked on arrival and it would make short trips to be closely parked for our own honed skills experience. Back and forward over a few yards. Never a scratch I recall. We soon got acquainted with all makes and models from Morris Minors to the more desirable Rovers and Vauxhall saloons

Less than convinced but desperate car owner in digs nearby remained unhappy, but paid up anyway. Plus it was cheap and handy. Not a problem as the other jobs around the garage and situations at hectic times soon developed into the opportunity to drive on the road. The trailer vans had to be hitched onto the Land Rover, up Bonny and Victoria Streets and driven across the main road onto the slade and sands of Central Beach. It was a sturdy short wheel base model with canvas top removed for most of the summer while the sun beat down. It also had the essential four wheel drive. An absolute treat to slide into a low gear and churn through a patch of soft sand that would have bogged down any other vehicle. It was soon to become my passport to driving short distances on probably the busiest stretch of road in England in summer-the Blackpool Promenade. What a place to learn to drive at nearly sixteen. Naventi's, a truly special resourceful Italian family business run by four daughters and their children from Bonny Street near to the Central Rail Station with a petrol pump and garage storage few yards further down. It was behind the long gone Victoria public house on the promenade adjoining the site now of the Central car park.

They had a full time driver in strong Glaswegian Jock Mackrell, a real character of the time who was very talented in maximising the times the trailers could be on the sands as the tide lapped the wheels. Vital for the continued selling of cornets wafers and orange drinks to what would be endless queues at peak holiday periods on sunny hot days. Only minor problem was he liked a drink and a bet on the horses and often to excess and the cutting fine of the timing to get all the vans off as the high tides raced in, sometimes causing a near disaster. He had his own white and blue liveried Land Rover with the newer one driven only driven by Gina the youngest sister. But she also served ice creams on the main and busiest trailer van right in front of the Tower, so not available at times like this. I would have been sixteen and now six foot tall and with the standard blue jeans and shirt and sunglasses, topped by the obligatory Tony Curtis hair style, could have passed for a bit older. Car driving licence and insurance not a big consideration with the quick decision on one emergency Bank Holiday.

Jock was late pulling one van off but the last one in front of the Woolworths building was about to be submerged as the westerly wind increased and brought the tide in quicker. Good viewing for the thousands packed on the sands in deckchairs, but no mobile phone camera's in those days to record the action. 'Well it's only a few yards up the Prom and down the slade at Central' said Virgie Naventi eldest sister and decision maker and I was soon behind the wheel and the rescue took place.

Got my full motorcycle licence soon after and the new earnings wealth ran to owning a rather dodgy but reliable enough BSA C11G 250cc motorcycle for transport. All paid for by working What a difference a couple of years make.

Chapter Three

Did not make too much of a habit of this law breaking and soon enough I became a full licence holder soon after my 17th birthday and passed my test for four wheels in a 3 ton Bedford truck courtesy of my then employers JT Youd and Son, Wholesale Grocers of Station Road. Only one achieved GCE when I left grammar school in, what else, but Geography with a near miss on History. It was not really the entrance qualifications to the dreamy spires of Oxford. So the few months up to seventeen and the world of drinking not smoking but playing snooker, having a bet on the horses had to do. Being a van driver's mate at the wholesale grocers and the summer and weekend's as varied work for the ice cream family business kept me busy and most of all happy. What did I need a day off for? Paid Mum the board money without being asked and for the first time used to give her extra when it came my way. Such as a win on the horses.

Eric Collinge Bookmakers on Bonny Street, on the exact site of the now Central Police Station had become a regular haunt with me and my mates who were developing our arithmetic skills far quicker than at school and working out multiple betting odds on such as Round Robins and Yankees. An established practice was the mugs double. You linked two horses together that had a name association. Geography again, as I spotted Atlantico and Pacifico running at different meetings and lashed out above my normal shilling or two shilling win bets.

I went for 2/6 pence each way on each with 2/6 pence each way double. Total bet 15 shillings so 75p in today's money. Both won at 4 /1 and 8/1 and reckon my winnings must have been around £7 something?

Serious stuff and a hazy memory that I might have given some of the winnings to Mum but with the expected 'Don't get into the habit of doing that. You won't always win'. Within days I was probably asking for a ten shillings sub to keep me in training at the Mere Park hotel where I had been picked for the semi snooker team. An important match was looming. We only ever went in the vaults that had the smaller snooker table, never the posh lounge with full size table. Arthur was the landlord for years and at around 6pm on a Friday the vaults were always full with lads off the building sites with the workers from Duple coachworks and Burtons Biscuits on Vicarage Lane. Several pints from damaged wage packets before the stagger home full of Catterall & Swarbricks local brewery mild and bitter. Never a wine glass in sight. The drinking days and smoking arrived slowly for me. The Woodbine cigarette at school at the back of the bike sheds never really was part of my scene, but when I was working full time after leaving school this became a way of life as it did for most, with the odd pint here and there and certainly an established Friday night and weekend meet up with friends.

The generally accepted social and then dependence drinking as I now refer to it, started to be very much part of me and was to remain for nearly thirty years.

So life was coasting along nicely and my personal transport had improved with buying another motorcycle from Bill Gregory's of Red Bank Road. A Triumph Tiger 100 twin 500cc, always second hand of course and along with friends from school, the first rides out around Blackpool and the Trough of Bowland and the more adventurous day trip to Oulton Park motorcycle road races near Chester. We tended to keep contact most weeks by the established place and times-the pub. None of this mobile and text nonsense or having telephones at home except for the few. The call round to each other's house by chance and the new haunts of the Mecca ten pin bowling club on Central Drive. Following a few days in North Wales at the now fashionable Butlins holiday camp drinking potent black velvet and bird watching, five of us even managed to arrange a lads week long holiday on the Norfolk Broads.

How we ever got there and back safely remains a mystery and the kindness and trust of Bill Taylor's mum and dad in lending us the family car to make the journey was quite something. By this time Barrie Oughton had moved back to Barnsley with his family from grammar school days, but we all kept some sort of letter contact. One of us had the bright idea to re live the 'Three Men in a Boat Story' by Jerome K Jerome. Not that we would have known of Mr Jerome at the time, but the plan was hatched with unsuspecting boat hire company based in Great Yarmouth to foolishly entrust us with the six berth 'Silver Song' for a week long cruise on the fabled and peaceful waterways to Oulton Broad and

Reedham being names I remember. Departure day dawned that summer and early start to pick up Barrie on the way in Barnsley and the long journey without motorways to Great Yarmouth. We had money for drinking. We did not have a clue about what food we should take on board, or any forward planning at all. Just get there, cast off and have a good time. Always the prospect of chatting up crumpet perhaps and luring them on board for canapés and refreshments. We did get there unscathed and picked up the boat in Great Yarmouth and sort of half listened to instructions on steering, engine start up and controls, mooring when in the tidal reach, observing speed limits to avoid creating a wash for other boat traffic. Plenty of common sense and off we went along the River Yare to find the first towpath pub...within half an hour we noticed the boat owner waving frantically to us at a bridge ahead. We had set sail without the essential mooring ropes. He had managed to track us in his car and the vital ropes thrown down to us as we passed underneath the bridge.

We all stood at in the bows and witnessed a commotion ahead. The strange sight of a yacht owner some 50 yards further along dancing it seems with rage, shouting hysterically and arm waving as we approached on full throttle ahead. His pride and joy was hauled up the river bank with his family taking a picnic alongside and it looked like he was clutching, what we later guessed was a large pot of varnish paint. It then struck us that the creaming bow waves we were creating would be greeting him and his beloved craft shortly, and that the big red circular signs we had been seeing on the bank with 'SLOW 3 MPH MAX' did have a meaning.

Somehow we survived the week without too much falling out. Several hangover's and by the end of the holiday, a loss of interest all round to be captain and in charge of steering the boat. I can also report the crumpet and luring aboard achievement result was nil-not that we did not try very hard. Back home to Blackpool and not long before John Gledhill, Bill Taylor and Dave Miller all had steady girl friends and I was sort of outside the inner circle and missing something... I was becoming more of a regular at the Mere Park pub for a couple, or more, pints most nights and the attraction of snooker which was improving to me racking up double figure breaks and certainly a guaranteed team place. Blackpool FC would be in their glory years but football, cricket and other sports had little interest for me. Girls did, but it seemed like I struggled to progress in that direction, but another event changed that as well.

Shirley Heeley who lived in Poulton and also worked at Naventi's I had known for some time and was a girl who I fancied, but sadly for me nothing happened other than being a friend at work. She had a girl friend from school called Linda, who called in one day when I was in the ice cream factory to look for her. We just got chatting and within a few weeks had been to the pictures a few times. Found out she lived with her Mum and younger sister Pat in a bungalow in Cleveleys and that her Dad, Alf Welsby, worked away for long periods around the world as an engineer in the power station industry for Babcock and Wilcox. At the time he was in China and then after some home leave, would be off again to Chile, South America for probably a six months contract. The pillion trips out followed on my Triumph Tiger 100 motorcycle with restrained parental approval of course. Linda was working at the Nat West bank on Victoria Road in Cleveleys and my van journeys around the Fylde Coast just happened to coincide with dinner break meet ups. One thing always stuck with me as the weeks went on and I was invited to the family home to pick her up in the van, or on the motorbike. She repeated to me that her Mum had said 'You can do better than a van driver can't you?'

Chapter Four

The early Bill Haley influence with the music scene was about to descend on us all with the Rolling Stones and Beatles but my route in life was about to change with a casual remark from friend Robert Simpson, again from Grammar school days, who was living with his parents in Toronto Avenue, Bispham: 'I saw John Gledhill the other day' he said. 'Reckons he is doing OK with the Police Cadets and told me they are looking for more officers to join'

The next day I was van driving round Blackpool as usual with plans soon to go and see the new James Bond film, Dr No, just released and being shown at the Odeon cinema on Dickson Road. Before the day was over I had parked up on Talbot Road and called in to the TA Barracks which I had been told had a recruitment office for the Blackpool Borough Police, to get an application form. That was the start of some life changing years for me that seemed to accelerate without any of this 'must have a long think about it' and 'am I doing the right thing'. Just seemed very normal to react to an opportunity that appealed-perhaps triggered something that was lurking anyway. Mum was very supportive as always when I mentioned my interest she agreed, but with a natural concern knowing perhaps that 'A policeman's lot may not always be a happy one.' She was proved right on that.

I have long been a reader of quotes and many I use today to remind myself that most things have indeed happened before and that human nature is repeated over and over. My stock favourite in recent years is 'In the end we will remember not the words of our enemies, but the silence of our friends' attributed to Edmund Burke 18th century politician. Closely followed by 'An ambition in life should be an objective-otherwise life, does indeed become an aimless wandering' That one from the supposedly grumpy Alfred Wainwright the original Coast to Coast walker. Finishing with 'Life is not measured by the years that we lived, but by the love that we gave and the things that we did'. Helen Steiner Rice. American poet of emotion.

To squeeze in a Northern offering that was passed down over the years. 'Yon man wouldn't know a good turn if he fell over one'. I did not have these quotes to hand in the sixties when the prospect of engagement and marriage loomed, or indeed can remember really just what I was thinking about and what I wanted. Peer pressure is a later life expression to explain actions but I would have found it difficult to stand up and be counted then and think clearly as to exactly what my life should bring and what I wanted. Oh, how I wish I could have been more determined and not caused the hurt that I did. Not an excuse, just a memory recall.

The application form was filled in. Within a week or so I was given a medical that confirmed I was apparently fit and well – at 6 foot tall and around 10 stone, I was 2 inches over the minimum height required for Blackpool Borough Police. Amazingly I had a clean full driving licence for motorcycle and car. References taken and background checks done, I was on the wait list for a few weeks. I was interviewed by an Inspector and asked reasons for joining and a general sound out I suppose with a letter following soon after to say I was accepted. In late 1963 I got the call to go back to the Police stores at the TA centre on Talbot Road and was told my force number was PC 287 and measured for my uniform. The sort of 'Heartbeat' style you see on television now was the clothing style and proud I was to wear it. The night helmet was black badged and the tunic and trousers, winter greatcoat and cape were of superb quality. Dated apparel maybe, but I never forgot the words of the retired officer who ran this department who said 'Listen son, this outfit puts you above some of the scum you are going to deal with. Most will respect the uniform...not necessarily you in it. So never be frightened-or if you are, don't show it'

Then came basic training for a three month spell at Bruche near Warrington. A police unit now long gone that had some two hundred plus recruits from northern forces, in five classes with trainers seconded from around the country. I really enjoyed my time there better than any forced school lessons years before. My class group just happened to be with the newly pro-moted Inspector Peter Russell from Blackpool Borough, not that any favours or even recognition of me was shown. In fact he went out of his way to raise the bar because of it I reckon. An accommodation block with some six beds or so to a room and a heavy work load of theory and practical classes. Our class had three women police officers, with Monday to Friday course work that was full on with an hour or so journey back to Blackpool late Friday's. Easy enough as I got lifts in cars or on the train.

One of the first trips out was to Warrington Morgue to see a dead body on a slab. Elderly female as it happened. For some it was the first sighting of death and that included me. Different reactions and some near faints, but get used to it were the words spoken. You are going to see plenty of that with blood, open wounds and bits missing. Weekends were short but I was seeing Linda more and I suppose the word regular girl friend was in place. The police social club on site at Bruche was typical of any pub lounge bar and the odd pint of beer taken some evenings -but any excess would have been frowned on. Most of all was the pressure of homework, so most nights were spent reading coursework. Several of the new recruits from other forces were a few years older having been in the army for a spell. Some good friendships made and the marked difference in background and attitude between a Cumbrian officer whose future customers would probably be farmers or from small towns, to the inner city one from Liverpool or Manchester force dealing with a large mixed city population.

The three months passed quickly and finished with a passing out parade and I got good theory marks which was expected back at Blackpool HQ. The town itself was hitting the headlines some two weeks before my return, when the Rolling Stones performed at the Winter Gardens Empress Ballroom and a near riot ensued. The more obvious street wise knowledge came fast when

I returned to Blackpool to as PC 287 Central Division foot patrol. Initial 8 hour shift of earlies, lates and nights, were always with the experienced PC's and what a bunch of characters they were. Bob Crompton was the newly promoted shift Sergeant and I spent many of the next few weeks walking the beats with Dick Moss and Dave Taylor who knew the town centre inside out. Time now for some name dropping. I had been back from training school for a few months and now out patrolling the various beats alone. Several small incidents dealt with and so far so good when one evening I reported in for the late shift of 4pm to midnight and as usual paraded in the staff room at HQ on South King Street where the sergeant assigned the patrols and updated us on any incidents or property needing a focus.

Myself and another officer were taken on one side and told we were to be at the Opera House at the Winter Gardens at 6pm to report for special duty as extra backstage security for the Beatles who were arriving then for a one night show. Just like that. By late afternoon probably every teenage girl for miles around was literally swarming round the building and for those with seats in the largest theatre in the UK an absolute bonus. Beatlemania had arrived big time. Of course it was just in a day's work as I stood in the wings of the stage on one side as the four lad's trooped on and did their set. My brief from Superintendant Howe in charge of the security operation was simple. Stand as near as possible in the backstage wings, without being seen from the front of stage and block anyone, such as a sex crazed girl fan, from getting past you. I think they played all the chart hits of the time, but the screaming noise was so deafening that I don't remember hearing any of the songs. The moment the curtains closed escape plan went into action as they followed us in a line down the service access to a lower level and through a narrow route to the fire door as it opened onto Adelaide Street at the side entrance to the Winter Gardens complex. Timed to coincide with a large saloon car with no markings, to whisk them away to Blackpool airport and onto a waiting flight. Even then it was a close call, as a few savvy girls had spotted the car drawing up and suddenly as the fire doors burst open, saw four guys they dreamed about within touching distance, pushed into the open car doors as it raced off. We had been in position on stage some ten minutes before curtain up as they stood around quite relaxed and easy to talk to. It would have been no problem to ask 'Any chance of signing this programme lads' as we waited for the set to begin. Not that I even thought about acquiring a programme or a poster. Never crossed my mind, till years later when I realised I could have probably bought a new car by selling it.

Unfortunately that was the lighter side, as by this time I was recently married and living in a police house on Rodwell Walk, on the same Grange Park estate where Mum got her council house years earlier. This part of my story I do not wish to dwell on over the following six years, but important to tell as it did happen and a sad time for many and most of all our children, Judith and Stephen. The years went by and I left home leaving a seven and four year old behind and subsequently divorced.

Joining the police in the Sixties had a big advantage over other jobs as you got either a generous rent allowance that paid the average mortgage on a house worth perhaps £2,000. (Yes-that was the price of a new three bed room house in the area and just a dream for many to raise the deposit even), or the option of a good quality police house with free rent. The allocation of the house option made the marriage prospects decision easier I recall and ...well we did get married and the police house allocated and my life must have just gone forward in that direction.

But it was a relationship that just sort of started and my fault that I did not stand up and say no, I cannot go ahead with this. Any short lived grief would have saved the heartache that followed for others involved. Perhaps it was the infatuation of youth and being swept away with what was expected of me. That led to a marriage that was miserable for me because of my failure to try and make it work. I find this difficult to write so many years on, but I have to say sorry that I allowed it to go as far as it did to a church wedding and vows made that proved that they were just empty words. It was the expected route of marriage, but by this time I suppose any accepted Christian beliefs I had, did not include any further church attendance or desire to be included in any worship. It was not a feature of my life and even to this day it is no other than a principle of civilised behaviour that I recognise.

To carry on for now with the story telling of what else happened, as the sixties progressed. I continued to enjoy for the most part, the police challenges of being based at Blackpool Central that arose in the different seasons of the year. I saw life as it was and a rapid growing up. From the day to day minor traffic incident to going to a late night pub fight and seeing how others lived in squalid conditions. No doubt at all that my confidence increased, but always the feeling that the uniform I wore to stroll down the central reservation of Blackpool Promenade afforded me friendliness, respect or at the least, wariness from the majority. This was the reality and the words of the officer issuing the uniforms proved over and over -but he is not around today to view public perception of authority and just as well.

Colleagues over the years have been doing just that and then put in a life threatening situation within seconds. Blackpool Police and not forgetting local emergency services have seen tragedy and outstanding bravery over the years and none more than the rescues from the sea with loss of life to themselves. Most of all a memory etched in many minds, of the death of Superintendant Gerry Richardson who lost his life on 23rd August 1971 being shot after a robbery at a jewellery store in the town. A truly exceptional man who I was privileged to know in my early years at Central Division. To proudly use the descriptive words of his close friend, retired Chief Superintendant Jeffrey Meadows when he referred to a saying attributed to Mahatma Gandhi which could have been written specially for Gerry. 'I shall pass through this world but once. Any good therefore that I can do, or any kindness that I can show to any human being, let me do it now. Let me not defer or neglect it, for I shall not pass this way again' Jeff often quotes these words as he keeps the memory alive with his unstinting work for the Gerald Richardson Memorial Youth Trust. 'Gerry was an outstanding leader of men and an inspirational officer way ahead of his time'

Jeff Meadows – you could not have put it better.

That's what I have met in many situations in my life, when you find that special person who reaches out and takes you literally by the hand with guidance, love, help and common sense in any order. They take that extra step and have that unhesitating inner courage to do so. Just for the satisfaction of wanting to do something for a fellow being.

A lot of the day shifts in summer would be on point duty at the regular traffic hotspots of the New Inn on the Promenade opposite the Palatine Hotel and Central Station. Talbot Road and Dickson Road point where the North Railway Station taxi traffic filtered in with a nod and a flick of the hand and Talbot Square opposite the North Pier. Half hour on and half off with fellow PC working the same could be a boring eight hours, but usually a few lighter moments to break the day and the ever grateful older shopping ladies you stopped the traffic for to safely cross. Ideally, a younger one with a mini skirt and a waspy belt who smiled and blew kisses to you. Sex and it's distractions and suggestions has got a lot to answer for but it helped pass those long hours breathing in petrol fumes.

We usually had a good camaraderie with the regulars including the landau drivers and taxi drivers and the from time to time, regulation breaking such as overload of passengers in cabs at peak times, ignored by us with staring indifference. These same guys would have no hesitation in helping if one of the lads was in difficulty with a drunken arrest perhaps and a free lift up to the nick on South King Street. The vital knowledge round town especially on breaks from point duty was the brew shops who welcomed the coppers visits. From walking confidently down the street, to a split second slide into a café back door entrance was a practised art. No mobile radios in the early days of the sixties and contact was still made from the regular Blue Box points that you rang into Central from at the designated times. Like the one at Talbot Square across from the Tivoli Cinema at the Corporation Street and Market Street junction.

My summer standing around looking skywards in Talbot Square was interrupted one late afternoon by seeing a gentle spiral of smoke coming from the distinctive crown top of the cinema building. Here we go again – me and fires, not that I would have thought that at the time. The spiral became a denser plume in seconds as I went across to the call box. 'Blackpool Police' said regular switchboard lady. 'It's 287 here – looks like a fire inside the Tivoli building. Am going to have a closer look.' The big red button would have been pushed as a major alert, as the full squad turned up within a minute from the Fire Brigade HQ on Albert Road half a mile away. Into the arcade underneath I went and saw cinema staff already at work with fire hose and most important the cinema was closed and nobody inside. But there were animals in the adjacent arcade pet shop and instead of a short Gazette report of 'Driver takes Vehicle Fire to Fire station in Fleetwood' a year or two back, I get my picture in the paper this time with small dog under arm – quote: 'Animals being rescued by police as fire sweeps through building'.

Not quite, but many years later when the whole block including Yates Wine Lodge was burnt down, my granddaughter Amy was shown the picture in the Gazette from 1964. We did a follow up visit to the scene for the Gazette when they dug the original story out and when asked by the journalist if she thought her

Granddad was brave all those years ago she replied 'I was just pleased the puppy dog's life was saved.'

My using the police call box at the time outside the Blackpool Town hall in Talbot Square was just one more of the lifelong what I call 'people and places revisits'. That unreal feeling at times of events that take you back perhaps only in the memory, or actually being there again years later. I still find it uncanny. Which then reminds me of another tale at the same call box some months after the fire incident in 1964.

I was on nights and waiting near the box to ring in to make the usual contact to switchboard-and probably before the first personal radios were issued. An unmarked Ford Cortina CID car drew up containing two Senior Gods, known to myself and everyone else in the force, as DC Jim Williams and the newly promoted Inspector Bert Stillings. Three years earlier they had featured in every national newspaper and had widespread TV coverage, when they arrested James Hanratty in the Stevonia Café on Central Drive. He was subsequently convicted of the infamous A6 murders.

The car window was wound down and I got the beckoning finger. I went over and the following conversation took place.

'How you doing lad. It's John Featherstone isn't it. 'About six months now from training school' I would have replied warily: 'Good on you' he said. 'Suppose you will be thinking of the future and what division you want to make a move to. Have you thought about joining us in CID for instance?' At this point Bert Stillings leaned across with a smile and said:

'Oh – just remembered, I have been drawn against you in the next round of the snooker knock out competition next Friday in the social club. Heard that you have been knocking a few breaks in son.' Reply from me something like 'Yes sir, been going OK in the first rounds, so will have to do my best if I'm up against you.' I was only just starting to twig then what the visit was really for, from these two legendary force officers and renowned law unto themselves. 'OK leave it with you John and have a good think about your career prospects won't you' said Jim Williams as they drove off into the night laughing.

A few lines of dialogue that would have done justice to a later Denis Waterman or John Thaw script in The Sweeney TV series. Not sure what I was thinking when the snooker match took place and my thoughts of not taking a dive, but it was close I remember and he did end up winning fair and square anyway. I even managed to remember to tell Bert Stillings the tale when in his early eighties, he attended a police reunion a few years back. The puzzled smile was back again and he said. 'I wouldn't have said that, would I?'

I was living two lives in a way. Without dwelling on the rights and wrongs, I had clearly agreed to marriage without long enough to decide was it right for me. I was drinking quite regularly perhaps to escape and to face up to reality, but then again it was so easy and sort of socially acceptable and I was able to put off any decision. Not an every night thing because the shift work meant that two weeks out of three on lates and nights it was only on the two days off before the next shift change. Certainly on early turn and having to be on morning parade for six am start did not lend itself to drinking much the night before.

But another danger lurked-the growing practice of the home brew beer and wine kits. Relatively cheap and a lot of kitchens or sheds would soon have a plastic drum or firkin or two frothing away. The quality and fermentation skills were in doubt but it was available and often potent. The age old excuse 'Alright if I pop down the pub for a swift half and see the lads'. Which actually meant a minimum 3 pints swallowed in double quick time, was not the best of ideas so the home brew was the hobby and an easy false world of escape. I was doing well in the police it seemed in my probationary two year stint at Central. A few arrests and secondment for several weeks training to traffic, plain clothes duty and the prosecutions dept to brush up on law and typing skills for incident reporting. Good reports at sergeant and inspector level and before long I applied for and passed my motorcycle pursuit test with an experienced traffic sergeant closely followed by the Class One car test in a Ford Zephyr which was the fleet choice at the time. I enjoyed it and in a way grew in confidence at work dealing with the public from the other world I had stopped breathing in -especially to my own private one I could always escape to. Might also be the one that carried severe hangovers, but it seemed to help and pretend and this went on for some time. Later concerns of the word dependency and alcoholic would not have been something to worry about, but then again I was finding a solution that suited me at the time. I was drifting away from friends I made at school who all seemed happy and settled – but I found solace in work.

I mentioned seeing the James Bond film Dr No and the idea of that lifestyle came to me when I picked up the Police Federation magazine during a break and saw the ad. 'Single officers invited to apply for Bermuda police with automatic achievement to the rank of sergeant/inspector on exam qualifications.' Not sure about the wearing white shorts bit, but I saw the word single and put the magazine down and did what I was able to do much easier. Put it out of my mind and think about it tomorrow.... Judith was born in 1967 and Stephen in1970 and by this time we had moved to a brand new house on Pinewoood Avenue, Bispham. One reason was the independence from the tied police house and I was transferred to the Bispham station as the traffic patrol officer to cover the more outlying areas such as Grange Park. The pattern that follows me over and over again by design, or whatever to see the same people and places popping up-and still going on to this day.

The patrol area in the main covered the large Grange Park housing estate that I knew well and certainly in the sixties there was nothing like the social problems that beset society today. There was one house that was receiving regular visits from the newly formed Drug Squad. Reality was probably that a DS and DC from the CID had been seconded to this role and at the same time learning day by day themselves of this new menace. I remember being involved in some minor domestics at the house when two otherwise normal teenagers were in another world so to speak. I would never have thought of the impact it would have in the years to follow at all levels of society. An occasional dispute at the now defunct Dinmore public house on the estate, minor traffic accidents in the main because few had cars and the rest of the time hopefully peaceful. I probably did around 100 miles a shift over 8 hours at three speeds. Mostly dawdling around the streets of the estate at around 20mph on one of the 3TA Triumph 350 cc twins we had on allocation at Bispham station and spending time car and people watching at roundabouts or on the Queens Promenade. The second speed was to keep to 30mph in the traffic and concentrate that I was doing everything the Highway Code dictated as others would be watching me for any failings. The last speed was flat out when you got the emergency radio call and the blue light went on. Buzz time-usually to an injury road traffic accident but sometimes on evenings or nights, to a burglary, fight or suspected car theft in progress perhaps.

Not quite the Isle of Man modest mountain circuit laps I did on Suzuki's later on, but still was able to arrive on scene pretty quick The radio handset was mounted on the tank with the three call signs for the bikes BQ 33, BQ34 and BQ 35. Strangely enough I struggle to remember my car number now but HFV 35D in 1966 was the latest motorcycle plate to coincide with radio call sign number BQ 35 and just that bit quicker than the other two last year models. Trivia bits of the memory, but then again I can still see the bikes parked up now. A similar picture showing the correct sixties era television series 'Heartbeat' period uniform with Corker helmet and wide gauntlets and identical bike with police man alongside appears in the Ladybird book for children called, naturally, The Policeman. A Christmas present for me snapped up by daughter Jude a few years back in a charity shop, with sticker she posted on the page and arrow pointing to 'xx My Daddy xx'. She still calls me 'my daddy' as her 50th approaches and hope she always will for a long time to come.

Chapter Five

The Bispham posting in many ways accelerated a few decisions. Without being too flippant it was run in a way similar to a private club that resented interference from the outside world. Or to be more exact-Central HQ. There was also a pride that whatever arose could be dealt with by the experienced officers in place. There was the usual variety of incidents for us to deal with and being a larger proportion than the central area of retirement residents living in bungalows and flats the local officer patrolling on his bicycle was a welcome site for many. The officer in charge of the twenty odd or so PC's and Sergeants was a kindly fellow coming up to retirement – Inspector Maurice Atkinson. He had a distinguished career I understand in all branches of the service and wanted his territory to run smoothly without a hint of interference from above. In the main it did. I wrote a short story some years ago to illustrate a true life event that sums up the attitude and policing at the time and filed it away. Seems like a good time to bring it back to life.

TEA AND TOAST – BUT NO SYMPATHY

One very large police constable was straddling the top of the larch lap fencing. Another was attempting to hand him a bicycle. A third officer was standing on a dustbin just about to drag himself over into the alley-way beyond.

To no avail – the great escape was foiled

* * * * * * * *

He was a bank manager from Harrogate and his mother lived alone in a northern seaside town some ninety miles away. Nothing much ever happened there in winter in the 1960's-a quiet avenue where most of the mainly elderly residents, went their own way in a comfortable state of retirement.

In the summer months it was different. A group from Liverpool called the Beatles paid their first visit and more infamously the Rolling Stones caused havoc at the Empress Ballroom dance hall with a resultant baton charge by the boys in blue to quell trouble. Z cars was on television and in real life the police had been issued with personal radios and Panda cars took the constables on patrol in town centres. In bungalow land to the north of the resort, progress was slower. A bicycle mounted constable from the sub division station was the primary way of enforcing law and order. He dealt with most matters and reluctantly, would ask for assistance from the CID and traffic divisions if the situation demanded. Central HQ was treated with suspicion and a level of interference to be avoided.

Perhaps the quietness was on the bank manager's mind when he called at the local police station one day and saw the officer in charge.' Would it be possible for one of your chaps to pop in and see my mother from time to time' he asked 'She's active enough for an eighty year old but rarely goes out now and – well quite frankly, I worry about her'

'No problem sir.' Was the reply from worldly wise constable and stalwart of the force. 'Thanks so much-I'm not able to call as much as I would like and I'm sure she would be pleased to offer a cup of tea and some very special sponge cake she makes.' Confident assurance of 'just leave it to us-that's what we are here for sir' was the reply.

Details left and off went the visibly relieved son to the world of finance with a promise to call in on his next visit. There was a note waiting for the late shift reporting for duty at 2pm. 'Who's on three beat then?' asked the duty sergeant. Request was passed on and sometime later that afternoon a police bicycle was propped against the wall of an immaculate bungalow and a visit was made to check if this lady was OK. Indeed she was and delighted to see the uniformed young man.

'Have you got time for a cup of tea and perhaps a slice of toast?'

'Well, certainly – can always find time for that' said the officer. Helmet and bicycle clips swiftly removed and in he went. He was shown into the homely, neat kitchen by the diminutive lady with the short white hair. He was sat down and the best china appeared with a flourish. The grill was lit and within minutes he was enjoying the most perfect buttered toast. Turned out she had been widowed for a number of years and though friendly enough with the neighbours tended to live a somewhat reclusive lifestyle. Kept herself to herself as the saying goes and looked forward to visits from her only son when he was able to visit. 'Would you be able to find room for a piece of my sponge cake young man?' How could he refuse?

Sometime later, feeling quite full, he mounted his bicycle and set off to be seen in the world, with the words of the sprightly lady left ringing in his ears. 'If you or any of your friends want to call in for a cup of tea, then you are more than welcome. I am always up very early so please do-and thanks so much for calling'. And that's how it all started. The police have been accused over the years for failing to act with due diligence. Some might say they couldn't catch a burglar if they fell over one and all they do is spend their time hounding the poor motorist. You can never find a policeman when you want one and other such derogatory comments. One thing the lads at this local nick could spot was a golden opportunity not to be missed – and it wasn't.

The word spread very quietly at first. 'Ma' or 'Auntie' as she became code named started to receive regular visits. A 'brew shop' on a particular beat, especially a discreet one, was a haven in bad weather. One that could accommodate more than one police bicycle parked down the side of the bungalow was even better. Each day during the morning and afternoon shifts 'Ma' used to receive a visit. 'If you boys are out in all weathers from six in the morning you can call then you know.' The lads did better than that. They started calling about six thirty and two or even three of them from adjoining beats would be tempted to make a detour on the way out from the station and go together. Even the traffic motorcyclist who covered the most outlying areas would join the early tea and toast brigade. Life was good.

'Would it be a problem if we smoked?' No of course not and ashtrays provided and before long the betting slips were produced and the Yankee and Round Robin bets were being struck for the days horses. Inevitably when men get together and relax the odd swear word tends to slip out when it shouldn't and when this happened, it was greeted with much amusement by Ma. 'Oh-I didn't know that policeman could swear like that.' Well they could and they did. Nothing too strong, but not the sort of thing you would expect on a winter's morning in an eighty year old's kitchen with the air thick with cigarette smoke.

Perhaps up to three of them with jackets off, wolfing down delicious hot buttered toast with tea in china cups. Betting slips spread over the table and heated discussions with suitable adjectives, to describe the chances of the day's runners at Haydock Park...Someone at the nick had the sense to ask if she was being taken advantage of and if they were 'pushing it' a bit perhaps? It was left to the original constable who called to work out when it was suitable to make further visits.

'Well I do like a rest in the afternoon and I've got all my cleaning up to do'

So the word was passed around. Tea and toast for the early shift from 6.30 to 8.30 and then just tea or coffee served up till noon. No callers till 4pm and then tea/coffee and biscuits till 6pm. All agreed then? Must not take advantage of the old dear...By this time the neighbours were well aware what was going on and both adjoining bungalows and those opposite, had elderly couples who were absolutely delighted to have a crime free environment from what must have been the most patrolled street in the whole of Great Britain. And that's how it all started.

By this time bank manager son had called back to the station and discreetly made the station duty constable aware of how pleased he was that his mother was receiving such special attention. It was perhaps as well that the finer detail and language was not divulged...

This went on for several months, and even though the sergeants and the resident inspector based at North division would have known something was in place, nothing was ever said. It was recorded from time to time as just a constable's 'visit by request' in the station diary. Inevitably some of the constables got transferred to Traffic Division and to the CID so what better idea than to pay a visit back to 'Auntie' in their shiny patrol car. She would be thrilled to see her 'boys' again. On one memorable winter morning as dawn broke, the story goes that outside in the street was parked a Ford Zephyr traffic car, an unmarked CID Ford Cortina and a Triumph 21 patrol motorcycle. To complement this presence down the driveway rested three trusty bicycles. Amidst this in a small kitchen, an old lady would be busy serving tea and toast to seven or more. Personal radios tuned in to answer the call of duty should it arise, but the only airwaves would most likely be blue ones in the kitchen.

Her life really had changed and it was said that this new family she inherited where going a long way to keeping her alive and certainly active. Her grocery deliveries had increased dramatically to be able to cope with surges in demand. However all good things, they say, must come to an end.

Spring was in the air and not for the first time, there was no direct senior officer on duty in the division with coverage being taken by Central HQ. Not that that was a problem as far as the resident constables on the shifts were concerned-life went on in a calm well ordered way. The Inspector was on holiday and it was left to a newly promoted Sergeant based at Central to be in charge. He made his presence felt in no uncertain way.

All the police vehicles had radio call signs prefixed BQ. The traffic cars were BQ1 to 6 with CID, motorcyclists, dog vans etc. having call numbers up to 40. All the constables on foot patrol had by the early sixties personal radios and their force number was prefixed with a very predictable C for Charlie.

The call number that everyone at constable level wanted to know the whereabouts of was BQ10. This was the Central division Ford Cortina that usually housed the duty inspector or sergeant. This was the senior rank that asked for reports and what you where up to and why sometimes you were not in the place you were supposed to be…damned cheek of it.

It was just after 6.30am and still dark on this February morning on the best policed street in Great Britain. On the roadway was BQ 33, a Triumph 3TA twin 350 cc police motorcycle with lights off and radio switched over to personal set carried by the officer. Down the driveway three bicycles lay entangled with each other, resting against the wall. Inside the first slices of the day were being taken off the grill and the air was thick with language and the smell of toast. Tea was brewing in the pot…'Get a move on Ma. I ordered mine before him-have you put sugar in this?' Personal radio sets turned low but no mistaking the call sign and near sounding voice.

'BQ 10 on at central…Yes – Roger 10.'

The next spoken question went down etched in the memories of the four. 'He's not likely to come up here and check at this time is he?'

"No, don't worry-anyway, which one are we putting in to make up the Yankee" said the soon to be unwise one. Bets completed and suitably fed and watered, the lads were reluctantly putting on helmets and gloves when the unmistakeable voice of the new sergeant sounded loud and clear. 'From BQ10 – rendezvous request please with North motorcyclist BQ33.'

A moment's delay-and from radio room at HQ came '33-BQ 33 receiving over'. Four stunned faces. 'Oh shit-he must be on to us. Have a quick look outside' A peer through the front room curtains. Sure enough parked up across the road in the lightening sky was the divisional car. Decision time and step forward the reluctant motorcyclist hero of the hour.

'Well I'm pegged on this one-he's seen the bike on the road-I'll just tell him I called in to see if the old lady was OK.' Across the road walked the constable to the car, pulling on crash helmet and gauntlets and car window was wound down.' Morning Sergeant-just checking if the old lady who lives here was OK.' 'Oh yes' was the less than convinced reply. 'Anybody else with you' A moment's pause. 'No-just me' he said leaning onto the driver's door.

The sergeant reached for his cap on the passenger seat and made it plain he wanted to get out of the car. Every second's delay was going to be valuable. 'Might as well have a look then' he said. Both walked back to the driveway, at the side of the bungalow and were greeted to a scene that would have done justice to a film clip of the Keystone Cops. The sight was pure comedy-etched in the grey light of dawn at the bottom of the small neat garden.

One very large constable, with helmet comically pushed back on his fast perspiring forehead, was straddling the top of the larch lap fencing whilst another was handing him a bicycle-one already having been thrown into the alleyway beyond. A third officer was standing on a dustbin just about to drag himself over the fence and beyond. Three sheepish fellows must have said something like 'Morning Sergeant.' To no avail-the great escape was foiled. Each constable was told he was going on report and to resume patrol. There was still time to tell 'Auntie' after the sergeant departed from the crime scene that a little problem had blown up and they would be back. The news of the 'morning raid' travelled throughout the force. Most found it amusing, whilst others had little sympathy. The inspector of the division on his return from holiday was devastated and thought that it reflected on him. Well – it did actually. Some four weeks later each of the four was served with papers under the police disciplinary code and paraded in front of the Chief Constable in his office.

The charge was a form of dereliction of duty, to which each pleaded guilty and the fine was a day's pay. None of the officers involved went on to achieve a higher rank and the traffic motorcyclist officer left the force a year afterwards. The sergeant carried on in the force for many years but his actions had a mixed reaction from his colleagues.

You can have your tea, but don't expect any sympathy is perhaps the moral to the story. Hard to think though, that they were mentally scarred by, having a 'police record' to dent their career. Most saw out their service and drew the pensions. Some might say this was an unnecessary abuse of privilege and that the officers should have been patrolling the streets rather than drinking tea. They say you can never find a policeman when you want one, but then nothing changes...

The upside was that one very happy rejuvenated old lady went on to live for several years and still received visits from the police. It was back to the original plan though-just one police officer at a time. Never push your luck and don't get found out. Could there be another moral to all this?

Yes there is and to realise that when life deals out something of good fortune never take advantage. If you do, be prepared to take the downside. Oh -and live the moment as you write the story many years later. – *John Featherstone.*

This story and the news that the Blackpool Borough police were to amalgamate with the Lancashire Force probably determined a decision on my future. That could have meant a posting to any other town, but the prospect of even that slim possibility and a growing feeling of wanting a change in my life decided me. I had always kept in contact with the owners and friends made at Leonard Heys, the Blackpool wholesale supplier.

Within a few weeks the decision was made and I resigned and was on the road as a sales representative for Lancashire selling cycle and motorcycle accessories. The same shops I was making deliveries to some eight years before. As industry boomed, so did the two wheel market for work and leisure transport especially in such as Barrow in Furness and the dock yards employing thousands. Honda were appointing dealers all over the country selling the ideal go to work transport and Vespa from Italy doing the same with the scooter market. In the Cumbrian town of Whitehaven a young man called George Lloyd was repairing bikes and scooters in his parents shed in the back garden and out of the blue had a visit from the Honda representative for the North in George Hickman. A man of few words who had apparently had a clash of opinion with his local agent. 'From now on you are our Honda dealer for this part of Cumbria.' Just like that and George who became friends to many, including myself over the years, went on to dominate the market in two wheel sales in the North of England and Scotland. He is sadly missed by his wife Cath and all of us-a shrewd smiling tactician, great story teller and an absolute dynamo of energy.

The Early Years...

Shirley's Golden Boy,
aged 2 in 1945.

"Hello!
Paul & Leonie!

love John x.x.

Showing early signs of
being difficult...

Norfolk Broads holiday,
aged 18 in 1961.

With the one I owe everything to...
My mum Josie.

PC 287, Blackpool Borough, 1964.

62

Buster, mark 2.

Jan at Satterthwaite
Cottage in 1976.

Taking 'Martha' for a ride at The Farm Cottage.

Mallory Park on a Gilera Saturno.

Jamie Whitham of Suzuki
with Jude at TT.

Px200 2.5 times scale Vespa model at NEC 1982.

Chapter Six

I had given up the safety net of the Police but the wage and commission in these years matched it. Best of all I had a new company car, a Vauxhall Chevette for personal weekend use as well. Mortgage being paid, but never seemed to have any spare money. Clarkson's Travel and Freddie Laker who started the cheap weekend trips to Benidorm for £30 had to wait a few years for me. Another determining moment came after a few satisfying years back with Leonard Heys. I was making my usual weekly call on Vin Cunningham Motorcycles in Darwen to take orders for NGK spark plugs, helmets, tyres etc. when Vin said 'Have you seen this advert for a rep for the North of England and Scotland for Suzuki?' He held up the motorcycle trade magazine. And that started a whole new life change again for me. Upshot was that with again kind understanding from my employers who had taken me on for a second spell, I was soon on the train to London for an interview with Maurice Knight and Peter James Agg who had taken on distribution as Suzuki GB. I must have given the right answers and said I was the man they wanted and became a sales representative for them.

None of this sales development executive or business administrator titles of today. You were just the sales rep. They also had a major asset in a rider they had signed up called Barry Sheene who as many know became a PR superstar both on and off the track. So my humble little Chevette was handed back and I got the keys to a brand new Ford Consul V6 which a local bank manager or similar might have struggled to afford. Not that Maurice or PJ lashed out with a big salary but with commission I had sales that rocketed on Barry Sheene's celebrity endorsement. I was certainly earning above the average wage at the time but the saving account remained empty-I was living the moment. I had to stay away from home probably 2 or 3 nights a week to cover the whole territory, but that was how it worked. I also met my first real life work mentor in David Bardsley who lived in Romiley, near Manchester and already with Suzuki and Lambretta and was a few years older than me.

As the sales and company grew he did not want to do the longer distances, so covered the area near his home and the Midlands. It worked well and I learned a lot from him. He had the unique gift of the public school background to be able to communicate at all levels, a family motorcycle history with his brother Bran that made him accepted with the lads in the workshop, but most of all a respect from all his long standing contacts.

The valuable reference from Vin Cunningham, my time in the Police force and motorcycle patrol duty experience of life, I will always be grateful for –all good background experience and learning. I would like to think my developing confidence and industry awareness helped at my interview. No doubt I had moved up the ladder from a small turnover local supplier of goods to decision making that involved thousands of £'s with new motorcycle sales-but David Bardsley was there a few weeks afterwards to put the finer points of people skills into play. If anyone was foolish enough not to appreciate a good turn from him, then perhaps fortune never shined on them again. Worth thinking about that I reckon. Nobody should 'owe you' for a good turn, but it's rewarding for them not just you, to give one back if they can.

Before I was thrown to the wolves on existing dealer franchise visits, he arranged in my first couple of weeks to visit him at his home in Romiley and run through some scenario's. I will always be grateful to him for questions he told me I would come across from dealers such as. 'Have you got any red GT 250 cc in?' Find out for definite with the office and when the next delivery is. 'Don't say yes, you think Suzuki have them in stock. Say you are not sure, but you will find out'. 'Do not guess-you will be on trial with them you know. This is what you do. Ring him back, ideally on a Saturday morning first thing (it shows him that you work week-ends) but make sure you speak to him personally. Find out say, that there are two red ones in stock and one blue. Also, the next delivery from Japan will be in five weeks ok? Every chance he will buy all three off you'. That's how it works. Build a relationship-and earn a few quid more than you thought.

That scenario works in different ways. You cannot demand to be loved, understood or rewarded back in your working or personal life. If you have that relationship of true understanding that is unconditional-then you do not need a rule book to go with it. It should always be two way traffic of give and take and important for any relationship to survive. Best of all is when you share some ups and downs to test it and end up close and stronger for it. That was to come much later for me, but worth waiting for.

Time again for a bit of name dropping, that this time it has a twist to the story. I had not been with Suzuki more than a few months, when I got the call to attend a special meeting of a new model launch to be held at the Inn on the Park hotel in Park Lane, London. The new top of the range GT 750 model was to be shown to selected dealers and the trade press and Maurice Knight the Sales Director and P J Agg had just returned from Japan with all specification and price information. A prestigious location was called for and as hotels go, this was the one.

The night before I was to be at the hotel for the set up in the first floor ballroom area. The motorcycle was delivered ready built from the workshop, to the rear goods entrance late that evening and the first problem arose-no room to wheel it up the narrow curving service stairs. I managed to somehow wedge it in the service lift and was ready to push the button when next to me appeared a tall slim figure on the bottom step of the staircase alongside. 'Oh sorry – do you want to come past me?' No reply from a man perhaps in his sixties, very pale with thinning grey hair dressed in white trousers and a loose fitting white shirt without a collar (I always remember that bit). He did not speak, but stared a moment at me and then smiled at the gleaming machinery of the new bike for a second or two, slowly turned round and walked back up the steps. That was it. So who was that then I thought? – but nobody from the hotel staff around to ask. Back to my own struggle and finally after much sweating, got the bike upstairs and ready for the meeting next day.

Then it was the late night drive back to the Aerodrome Hotel on Purley Way in Croydon, where outside sales staff always stayed at during head office visits to nearby Beddington Lane. The room rate I recall was around £10 for D.B & B. The £60 a night room rate for the Inn on the Park was near enough a week's wage and certainly not an option for a mere mortal like me to stay at. Other than thinking on the drive back what a strange bloke I saw on the stairs... I just forgot about it.

Some weeks later the papers ran the headline that the secretive American recluse, Howard Hughes, had moved out of his penthouse apartment on the top floor at the Inn on the Park and supposedly flown out with his minders to the Bahamas. The report said that he had been there for several weeks but always kept out of public sight – except for me perhaps? So the question is, did I meet him and if not, who the heck was it who looked like him and was going quiet walk about at night?

The seventies were under way and life went on for me. Work going well and meeting targets and achieving bonus-and nearly always away from home travelling, that in a way kept a lid on matters as life drifted on with Linda and I. Judith by now some four years old and ready for school and Stephen who was two years in old in 1972. I loved being with them, but knew I could have been a bigger influential part of those growing up years if I was there more and inside wondering how long that was going to be. I was a bit more under control not overdoing the drink habit (it was actually an addiction by then, but I would not have realised it). The need was there, but so were all the problems of drink driving and the constant hangovers I really did not admit to.

But I was smoking less and probably thinking about eating healthier food but another far more important decision had to be made and I left home to live with my old school friend Barrie Oughton, who had a small open all hours type shop on a large housing estate in Leeds. He had a girl friend and was out much of the time. It was cheap. It was a bed in a spare room with basic facilities-it was an escape and without dwelling on more detail, I lived there for nearly a year with difficult weekly or fortnightly visits, to see two very frightened and puzzled children who had naturally pulled away from me.

Work was my saviour as I still travelled all over Scotland and the North with my constant evening only beer companion that included the magic sleep inducer of a swallow of Bells whisky to finish. A steady escape to the calming world of alcoholic problem solving to take away the reality and pain. An avoidance of contact with my family and other friends, offers of help and suggestions ignored ... to be the best that Suzuki had as a sales representative was easier to deal with and I continued to throw myself into that. Earn the money and pay the maintenance and mortgage on a world I had left behind. The continuing story below then leads onto the "what happened next" in my mixed up seventies

There was a life changing moment for me around this time. My sister Shirley was married to Ron Milburn and was at a Parent Teacher fund raising event at the newly opened Palatine School on St Annes Road and suggested I called in on a Saturday afternoon. She introduced me to her friend and neighbour Janet who, like her, had been expecting at the same time. Janet had three children and like Shirley, a few years older than me. That day I really fell in love for the first time... and NO, I did not get that line out of a film. It was the strange feeling of a moment of wanting to be with someone forever-that I had never even met before. I saw across the room someone I felt inside that I wanted to be with for the rest of my life. She was laughing and enjoying herself with other mothers, as she did her best to raise money for the school event. She was probably happily married I must have thought, so what was I thinking? I left soon after and tried to put it out of my mind. It did not stay out and remained in my secret thoughts, but the old unsettled feeling was back again with a vengeance. I knew so many others would be upset at whatever I did, or even dreamed of making happen. I just had to carry on and live in my confused world in which I did, never asking about her. Best to fast forward this story line and say that four years later with a lot of anguish for others involved, we did drive off to Kennerleigh Avenue in Cross Gates Leeds to set up home together on a cold grey morning on the 1st November 1975.

Forty plus years later Jan is my friend, counsellor and very much the love of my life.

As the seventies advanced, the sales of motorcycles increased and I did my very best to improve the Suzuki share along with Lambretta scooters already established in the north and Scotland. Appointing more outlets when opportunity arose and gaining the important trust of the dealers who sold them. Anything to get one across those rich types down south, who thought we all wore cloth caps. In Leeds, Eddie Wright ex GPO telegram delivery boy had opened his shop on the busy Kirkstall Road and before long was selling hundreds. I met for the first time Stuart Feeney who was working with Colin Appleyard in a converted terraced house in

Bradford Street Keighley and had just started selling the Suzuki range. The same ones who developed a multi million pound empire with Suzuki bikes and cars, but that day deliberated long and hard before giving me an order for one GT 750 priced at £ 799.50p retail including 10 % value added tax.

I met up now with the Isle of Man TT winning riders I had first seen hurtling past me as a schoolboy years earlier. Bill Smith and Tommy Robb from Chester, and then later Tony and Nick Jefferies from Shipley, Mick Grant, Phil Mellor and Jamie Whitham from Huddersfield and Phil Mc Callen from Northern Ireland. So many riders and characters, who naturally turned their race skills to starting as dealers, or just carrying on the family business. Local dealers Peter and Barbara Slinger of Preston who were churning out new Suzuki bikes to riders who travelled from many northern towns to buy from him rather than a nearer shop perhaps, because he was just Pete. The word "genuine nice guy" stamped on his forehead and an absolute pleasure to laugh and remain friends with.

As time went on I got to know Colin Mayo and Roger Willis, very sharp and experienced journalists and editors from the trade magazines and was encouraged to write to them on any debatable or insider issues, to be published on the reader pages. Sometimes to tread a careful path I became 'Name and Address withheld' or if the subject matter was not too controversial then 'Confused and Puzzled' was the sarcastic pen name. The contact carries on to this day with the utmost respect I have for Brian Crichton and the current editor of British Dealer News in Paul Smith. By this time I was a steady reader of classic novels of different genre and always lurking within was the desire within to write more than the odd page of comment or protest letter. I became very interested in the post WW2 and fifties style writing and thinking of Nevil Shute who had many of his novels such as " A Town like Alice" and the chilling tale of "On the Beach" made into films. I found another escape to read, reflect and understand past life better than what was the present moment of time for me. Perhaps the determination was there just below the surface to write more than just a grumpy protest letter to a magazine. Time again now for that return to the working past and friends and contacts.

The Suzuki sales were still going well and the two wheel travel and sports market that had been rising for the last four years was still increasing and I was approached to set up a branch for Leonard Heys Ltd who had strong distribution links in Greater Manchester and Lancashire, but none in the county of Yorkshire. Third time round is beckoning with this company. With regret and the decision was made to resign to a very understanding Maurice Knight at Suzuki. A job that was still taking me from my new home with Jan some two or even three days a week decided matters and by 1976 we had opened a motorcycle spares and accessories ware-house branch for Leonard Heys at Eccleshill, Bradford, with Jan running the office administration. Another development was that we had two new additions to sort of stabilise and help us in our belated late start in life at Leeds. The first was Buster Mark 2 – a crazy Springer Spaniel who was part of our lives for the next 14 years with his loyalty and unpredictable attitudes to behaving.

More meaningful is that I am proud to this day and always will be, of the very special help I received in those often stormy difficult times from a 15 year old. Jan's youngest son John who had the courage to want to come and live with us and uproot his life in Blackpool. In the next few years, this young man was my absolute strength, as he worked with me to establish the business and organise the staff at the branch. Talents surprising for a teenager who coped with the difficulty of a new home life, as well as changing school for the last year. So much of the immediate success of the branch was down to him and to this day whatever 'time to time' differences or opinions we may have, he will always have that special place in my heart for what he did for me in those important years. Harrowing times when I was close to going under and he was there to take over – and he did. Well done JD.

Chapter Seven

Fortunately there were the lighter moments to reduce the self induced stress of life. My friend Brian who had been a work friend at Leonard Heys in Blackpool, told us about a cottage to rent on a working farm at Dale Park, Satterthwaite some five miles from Hawkshead village in the Lake District. Very remote and most of all affordable and dairy farmers Roger and Ann Martindale ran the small farm in the old fashioned traditional way as Roger's family had for generations.

Jan and I, not forgetting Buster 2, (who thought he had arrived in heaven as he roamed free) rented it at Christmas. The first time for what I think was £ 27.50p for three nights and there after summer short breaks and week-long stays. Firewood included in the price. Those became the key words, as over that first biting cold festive time, we made a serious attempt to burn all the logs he had sawn for us from the surrounding Grizedale Forest. When we arrived a massive stack was piled by the door with a small box of kindling, which we thought would last for the whole winter. A simply furnished adjoining room to the main building, the

cottage as it was called, had two small upstairs bedrooms and a toilet/bathroom. We never even thought
of having a bath-it was too cold! We had taken changes
of clothes, that if I remember stayed in the suitcase or
we put on two or three layers to keep warm. We probably did wash our hands and faces and fed the electricity
meter that gobbled up 10p or 50 pence pieces for water
to do the washing up.

A short lane to the main road from the farmyard to
turn left to the Force Forge junction and the Eagles
Head pub in the village always beckoned. Or you could
trek straight across the forest for a mile or so on forestry
tracks, for the more direct route to the village and the
bonus of deer spotting if you were quiet enough. The
Eagles Head pub was the focal point of village life and
meetings with local residents Bob and Joan Fletcher. A
butcher from Accrington who opted out of mainstream
life and went to work for the Forestry Commission
based in Satterthwaite with a tied cottage in the late
sixties. He pursued his special skill at painting wild life
and running a sanctuary for injured owls and birds of
prey. Today he still has that unique talent and I am
proud to have an original of his work.

The main lounge/kitchen had the most fabulous large
open fireplace, so we thought that technically if you
burnt a few logs in the centre and kept them covered
with ash, they should gently smoulder and throw out
heat for the whole room all day and evening. Wrong!
No double glazing –no draught excluders and ice on the
inside windows. Third degree burns on face and hands
as you huddled over the crackling logs sitting on the
hearth with coats on and backside and feet needing
treatment for frostbite. This haven for us became a

welcome retreat for many years to come and a place where all our children came to stay at various times.

It gave the affordable thinking time of freedom to walk in the quiet Grizedale Forest area and reflect where life was taking us. We also came up with a one liner that we use to this day when a particular situation arises and the tunnel ahead seems very dark. 'So what are we going to do? The first thing is to find a way to carry on working and how to turn this to our advantage' Seems to have be the solution because staring at a wall and hoping that things get better is never the answer. I flashed my mind back to those days at school when I stared out of the window not understanding a particular teaching endeavour. The thought of French teacher 'Drip' Murdoch, the poor fellow, literally 'pushing treacle uphill' in life trying to teach and prepare us for what lay ahead in life.

I probably was doing my share of treacle pushing and repeating mistakes, but hopefully getting the important sights in mind to resolve one day. I also had late in life new parents in law called Mr and Mrs Herbert and Josephine Palmer who lived on Waterloo Road, Blackpool. Not that I called them that-nor did a lot of other people. He was Bert Palmer a long established stage, TV and film character actor well remembered for playing Alan Bates train driver father in the sixties film 'A Kind of Loving' along with an excellent cameo role in the TV feature film All 'Creatures Great and Small' with Simon Ward and Anthony Hopkins. Lots of TV series walk on parts with such as Morecambe and Wise, but most of all he was another talented painter and a kind and gentle man. New Mum also had a long career in repertory theatre following forces ENSA duty with

Bert, when they toured the country during WW2 in troop shows. Small TV parts and then one day in 1960 a train trip to Granada Studios, Quay Street, Manchester for a small part in a new drama about everyday life. The rest, as they say is history, as she became Martha Longhurst in Coronation Street (the busybody of the snug trio in the Rovers Return with Ena Sharples and Minnie Caldwell). One of the first of the cast to be famously killed off by dying on set, she more importantly never forgave the scriptwriter for denting her building society savings book plans for retirement. But she did have a great part a few years later in 1979 playing the same outspoken type of role as Annie in the film 'Yanks' starring a young Richard Gere. Both Bert and Mum supported us both with understanding and perhaps a little unease, along with my mother and Shirley from day one of our new life together. No criticism-just a quiet acceptance that this is where destiny as I called it, was going to take us. And not forgetting new brother and sister in law Bob and Julie who were in the RAF and lived in Lincolnshire. Equally close to this day to share many a memory.

It did strike me more than once that I seemed to make a habit of moving on and touch wood, landing on my feet-for a time at least! The essential effort I always tried to make in past jobs was to leave on the best terms if I could. Made sense to leave a door open if possible and depart as friends and that was certainly needed as 1981 approached and we had been there five years. The economy had been improving year on year through the seventies and branch turnover increasing at Bradford, but it was not to last. Decision made at Blackpool office with a steep downturn in turnover imminent as demand decreased and the decision made to close the branch. That left Jan and I and young John redundant. Disaster and we were wiped out for a while but – on we go and within months John had joined the RAF and I am back on the road with my old company Suzuki who have taken on the Italian franchise of Vespa scooters. Talk about being here before and going round in circles meeting the same people.

Also gave us the opportunity to sell the house we were buying and move back to Lytham St Annes, to the same bungalow we are in today some 33 years later. This is where you need friends to make it happen and family to support and they all did. A young Charlie Jagger, who had set up a motorcycle repair business in Shipley with his friend Lee Cobb and bought spares from us, helped me with immediate transport when the company car went back-a trusty loaned for free Honda 50cc step thru moped. Charlie today is the owner of a major motorcycle dealership in Shipley selling Ducati & Triumph and also qualifies for the title good friend in need. Then the phone rings and old friend and mentor David Bardsley comes on and says 'Put the phone down Feathers, you are going to get a call from London offering you the job of Vespa sales manager for the North and Scotland, so act surprised' Just like that – back again to what I was doing ten years earlier. Rescued from the dole queue and the opportunity to head back close to family and our home town of Blackpool and thanks to a lot of others I was back on my feet. What a lifeline I was given. Thank you most of all to David Bardsley – clearly a man who I can always think back to, with others who had no problem in stopping like a Good Samaritan to help. Perhaps still unsteady on my feet at times because that was something else I had to deal with. Putting this right and repairing an important relationship seeing more of two growing up teenagers who had drifted away-both needed attention.

Good times to reflect in a way to a life changing event when you are given the proverbial kick up the backside. It was just the focus I needed. I seemed to have an easy affinity to understand and develop a sales career in motorcycles and was natural for me to build personal relationships and trust on visits to franchised dealers around the county. Never technically blessed, but I did work out how to exploit the best results from each whilst trying to weigh up what the rest of life held for me. Perhaps ten years earlier was too soon to concentrate, but the return to Lancashire and settling into yet another home became the opportunity to decide – what do I really want? The obligatory 25,000 miles a year travelling was starting to bite on body and mind. What is the saying 'Be careful what you wish for' so for all those out there who perhaps think you have got a nice company car for personal use as well and stay in good hotels – well think again! What we did get was a chance to rebuild with the important issues that had nothing to do with being a success. Time to go together for long walks with Buster on the St Annes beach and in the countryside. When I say we, I'm not sure he was with us most of the time as he had this compulsion to go runabout in ideally far off sand dunes or deep forest dependant on location. We never found him apart from glimpses of a fast wagging rudder, but he always found us. Not least was the wonderful diversion and opportunity to become a dedicated greenhouse tomato grower.

What better than being located in the old glasshouse area of Marton Moss on the Fylde Coast that was the premier growing area for this fruit (vegetable) for many years. Getting the cultivation right can drive you mad but it became an obsession for me and has remained so for the last 30 plus years. If other challenges of life have defeated me, this one tops the bill. But the satisfaction of getting everything right in a good year and cropping tasty tomatoes from my 10 foot x 8 foot greenhouse is worth every hour spent. The special warm summer evenings in silence, when the television sets and lap tops are flickering in the surrounding bungalows and I am sitting alone in my own mini jungle on a light failing summer evening. It has a special reward. I think I am at peace looking at the sturdy ever thrusting upward plants with setting flowers and already ripening by the day tomatoes on the first truss.

I think of the pinhead seeds I germinated in February to start the life cycle, when I'm jolted into reality from my relaxing wicker chair. (The same one I kindly rescued off the council tip in Kilnhouse Lane years earlier and will outlast me). I incredibly see a small energy sapping side shoot growing off a main stem on one of the Shirley variety plants. It has escaped my attention and has to be nipped out immediately-and I am saying that I am totally relaxed and at peace? I might be writing this in a light hearted way, but other gardeners will know it does become a strange sort of relaxing obsession and solitude escape year on year.

'It was during those life is good' summer evenings in the greenhouse that recurring thoughts took me to a decision. Some four years earlier at around 40 years old, I had finally packed in smoking and amazingly was able to taste and enjoy food a lot more-but a more important issue lurked as the daily dependency drug was ever present. All I needed was a symbolic time and date to put the plan into action and it did not take long to settle on midnight that year end 31st December 1988. I decided I had to give up drinking alcohol for ever. I have a few months to get used to the prospect of being teetotal for the rest of my life. No going back. No announcement-just do it and I went out in style!

Chapter Eight

Jan and I were settling into our new home in St Annes after five years. Work was going well and holidays to the Cotswolds and ever increasing amounts of happy times being involved looking after our new grandchildren Christopher and Holly. School runs, trips to the beach and the retelling of stories that I had been brought up on. I was seeing more of my own two growing up teenagers in Judith and Stephen and generally the turmoil of the last years settling down.

I meet Steve Kenward, Ernie Hendy, Graham Goodman and Colin Pattison as I start my life again travelling round the UK, this time to put the iconic brand of Vespa back in the sales charts. In the fifties and sixties the Mods and Rockers had these and the Lambretta scooters as fashion statements and in the headlines for the wrong reasons. Suzuki was now Heron Suzuki and the well known new owner and entrepreneur Gerald Ronson was expanding his empire. Good times beckoned again for me as I met some very different characters this time round from the traditional motorcycle dealer. Same hobbyist background of some of the shop owners, but it became a bit 'pushing treacle uphill' to try and win confidence and widen sales appeal. Possibly they thought that all non-dedicated scooter only riders, were the enemy rockers from way back. Dave Webster and Norrie Kerr who started the very successful Midland Scooter Centre, both ex scooter racers who I took years to hopefully convince I was right about something. I still see canny Scot Norrie to this day at trade shows, as we attempt to put the world to rights. Their customers tended to be often cult followers who went to rallies, lived the soul music scene and still out to prove that mod fashion was alive and well. That was OK and probably sold up to a thousand scoots a year. Our brief was making it at least 5,000 and widen the market appeal as commuter transport. Steve Kenward was the newly appointed and very approachable sales director. New to the industry with a well qualified business back-ground, I have nothing but praise for all he did for me over the coming years. A genuine man, who, in a long industry career, is still juggling with live geese trying to please everyone.

Ernie Hendy was the original Mr Vespa from the importers Douglas Vespa based in Bristol. He became my partner and host barman in the hospitality suites of the many public and trade shows we went to together, starting with Earls Court and then the newly opened NEC arena. But we were non starters and upstaged big time on one occasion. The ones who were really ahead in the hospitality game in the motorcycle industry were Honda. Under the legendary and charismatic leadership of ace showman Eric Sully, they famously launched their top of the range Gold Wing tourer at the Metropole Hotel on site at the NEC prior to the opening of the annual motorcycle show. Market leaders Honda invited every single dealer in the UK with wife and partner to attend. The plan was to entertain with champagne and nibbles some one hour before the show opened and then all the dealers being full of joy and satisfaction and part of this world wide success, would march triumphantly together into the main hall of the newly opened show. A brilliant orchestrated idea.! Oh-and something else. Each was to be given a Gold, Yellow and Green shiny paddock jacket emblazoned with the words Gold Wing. Minor problem-the one hour reception over ran as, for the first time ever it was reported, the Metropole Hotel was cleared out of champagne. The one hour drinks reception dragged into two hours with hastily sought replenishment of other wines and spirits, plied upon willing guests. Time then for the grand entrance of some 300 plus paddock jacketed 'tired and emotional' figures to, stride with pride into the arena in an orderly column. Not quite. I and many others were treated to a comic and memorable show of seeing our well known industry dealer friends, literally strewn all over the stands with wrong sized jackets they had picked up at the last minute and with some still clutching a fluted glass of celebration. Oh happy days.

Graham ran the day to day operations of Vespa and had wide experience from his Suzuki dealings mainly in the south of the UK. Colin came from a different back-ground and his claim to fame was the marketing success of Action Man, every child's must have toy. With wife Shirley they played a dynamic role then and in later years, making Piaggio Group the Italian parent company, very successful in the UK market as widely used trans-port for all ages.

Another development was my involvement in the marketing of Suzuki and a return to my boyhood day visits to the Isle of Man. Blackpool airport is a 25 minute flight away to Ronaldsway airport, so once again back to old haunts-but this time in some style. No more overnight huddle in a rain swept bus shelter on Douglas promenade as a 14 year old. Flights out and all paddock passes arranged, with a quality hotel stay for a few nights to arrange with Colin the display of the new range of Suzuki clothing and support for the race team. This was led by Mick Grant and Rex White with the very talented riders in Phil Mellor and Jamie Whitham. The distinctive letter S for Suzuki had the new sponsors name of Durex alongside. Yes-that Durex, which was a big step away from the usual drink, fuel and cigarette sponsor companies that advertised on race machine and rider clothing as television increased motorcycle sport coverage.

Nice one Mr Kenward – you certainly handled the press release of the new sponsor in a most delicate way and within weeks we had tied up a deal with Top Shot promotions of Congleton, Cheshire and thousands of tee shirts and paddock jackets emblazoned with the red, white and blue Durex Suzuki logo's became very accepted leisure wear.

But the start of this enterprise goes back to TT week in the Isle of Man. Colin and I were manning a stand at the ever popular Creg ny Baa corner on the mountain circuit during a hot and sunny race day in the first week of June and the new product was on sale. Two middle aged guys who were not really switched on to potential race support sales to the public, we soon realised we were not the world's best salesmen. But we sold a few to the more adventurous lads and girls, who had no hang ups about wearing a Tee shirt with the word Durex on. In the crowd nearby I saw a very attractive young girl, late teens or twenty, long dark hair with the latest blue and white race lookalike Suzuki RGV machine, with matching coloured leather suit relaxing between the races. 'Have you seen her over there-that's what we need' I said to CP.

Chat up time was needed-which in reality was probably a stumbling attempt on my part to find out more about her. Where she lived, did she have a boy friend and ended up tamely saying something like 'See you're a big Suzuki fan. My mate and I reckon we need someone like you to be involved selling race wear at events. Could you be interested?'

Jane Swindells from Leicester joined us and with her friend Belinda, really did make Durex Suzuki a branding success going to many events with the liveried trailer they towed all over the country to race meetings at Brands Hatch, Donington Park, the North West 200 in Ireland and the NEC annual bike show. Memory says that we were at Brands Hatch and Barry Sheene took her on the pillion of his paddock bike for a ride round to make her day. Reckon you still tell that one Jane? Well done girls for those great years, but be careful in future if strange men approach you.

As 1988 drew to a close the decision date of New Years Eve was nearly with me. All continued well at home, we even had modest regular savings accounts and increased our pension funding. The government bless them, through the National Health Service were even hyping up the dangers of drink consumption and suggesting safe quantities. Even so far as suggesting you had at least one night a week off from having a drink, or better still several nights completely free of any alcohol. Ridiculous and unthinkable for me. That was not an option and I suspect many others to this day would also find it difficult. I just had to do something to get free of this dreadful addiction that I wanted to be rid of. Not to cope with my body telling me it needed a regular drug intake every day or so...

So the usual falsity of the season of good cheer arrived and this so called religious festival is upon us and into the last days of 1988. I have kept my thoughts to myself, which is difficult for me, as Jan and I have spent our lives sharing and talking. New Years Eve arrived and as usual we were at home and not planning to go out anywhere. I had secretly assembled my last stocks of several cans of Stones bitter, remnants of a bottle of wine and nearly a half bottle of Bells whisky, always kept sort of out of sight as proper drinkers do. Family visits during the day with probably a glass or two of wine or beer and then settle down for the TV and reading before bedtime. So far so good. Late meal and the washing up and I am pottering around as usual and around 11pm start my consumption of what is left. With minutes to go to midnight I do remember leaning (slumping perhaps is more correct) on the wall alone outside the back door at 45 years old, looking up at a cold starlit sky and finished the last drop from the bottle of Bells. 'That's it then Feathers' I would have slurred to myself 'There's no going back'.

A New Year's Day and a subdued house as Jan was certainly not pleased, as once again I had overdone the drinking. With a thudding hangover in a silent household, I forced myself to do some garden tidying up and found an empty Maxwell House coffee jar in the bin that was duly washed out and prepared for its new role in life and in it went a £5 note to start Plan B. The plan was simple and followed Plan A, which 26 years later is going strong. I have never had another alcoholic drink since minutes before midnight on the 31st December 1988.

The Plan B coffee jar contents with weekly additions were destined to pay for a £1,000 plus a year holiday every June for a week or 10 days at the Alpenrose Hotel Wengen in the Bernese Oberland of Switzerland. Mission accomplished and we have had 23 wonderful holidays so far over the years to the same hotel...A lovely family run retreat that we took 15 year old granddaughter Holly to some years back.

Not to say the first six months of 1989 were easy, as stubbornness and determination became essential friends to help me. It was back to work and hotel staying away from home most weeks for the odd night, that proved the hardest test of discipline. Apart from Jan who helped me with quiet pride for what I was doing, nobody knew of my decision for many weeks and I kept away from any social meet ups when possible. I always carried the Maxwell House jar with me in the boot of the car and always added a few pounds, especially when the desire for drink was strongest. Would sometimes wake in the early hours, to have a reassuring count of my new found wealth saved and to make the inevitable cup of coffee or snack eat to keep the resolve going. I started a journal of daily achievement and wrote in words to encourage myself and how I was damned if I was going to give in, as the days became weeks and into early summer. Always tried to look forward to the hours to be spent on long walks, or in the garden in all weathers as I spent hours driving and thinking –I cannot and must not give up now. All the weeks of effort would be for nothing – reach for another chocolate bar, or park up in a service area and phone home to hear a supporting voice telling me she is proud of me. It worked and on my birthday in June six months on, the nagging reminders of want became less and less. Then they stop for ever.

Not that I would ever pretend to this day that to have a single alcoholic drink would be OK. Quite possibly it would have no addictive effect, but then I could never want to try, or even be tempted. One or two friends asked me later how I relaxed after stressful work days for instance without having a drink. Easy was the answer-I am still capable of falling about laughing after hearing a funny well told story for example. Before I used to just fall on the floor...

There was also the very satisfied feeling of flying out from Manchester to Zurich for a week in June and the superb scenic train journey onward through Berne and Interlaken, culminating in a fantastic week's holiday walking, eating and sleeping soundly in the mountain air at the Hotel Alpenrose Wengen. All paid for with diverted income. Sounds self congratulatory perhaps, but what the hell. The memory of that first special Swiss holiday has stayed with us forever. I would suggest to anybody who is suffering within and can find the strength to press the release button-do it. To this day alcohol has the title 'Poison' for me -or at least the toxins within it are. If my metabolism or whole body reaction could have been tuned differently perhaps and with it, the disposition to enjoy the proverbial glass of Rioja wine with a meal from time to time, then fine. To be or not to be? For me it was never the question.

Chapter Nine

Need to do something else with my time, energy and thinking of the future I reckon as selling motorbikes, scooters and growing tomatoes can be a limited process and the creation of glazed eye reactions from friends and family. Mrs Thatcher had arrived to rule the UK and with it the idea of privatisation of state owned companies. Having thought for years that Viv Nicholson of Castleford probably got it right with Spend, Spend, Spend when she famously won £75,000 on the pools and lived for the moment – I decided it was time to wake up to increasing middle age and think what next? The stock market perhaps? All this advertising from above of the man in the street sharing in Britain's future. To dabble and find an opportunity to plan ahead without too much capital risk. A few years earlier and my modest Skipton building society balance would have been below the minimum possibility of buying any shares. Time to research and mother in law came to the rescue with an opportunity to get on the ladder.

Being an Abbey National account holder in 1989 she qualified for the standard £100 free shares and the opportunity to buy more. Out came the faithful Maxwell House jar and a further £100 purchase was made. Memory says that within a year or so they had more than doubled in value and we sold them. I was on my way playing in the big league. Soon after we saw an ad in the local Gazette for evening classes at the local high school on the heading 'Introduction to buying and selling on the Stock Market'. My new interest in life had arrived and I literally threw myself into research and concentrated study in a classroom that was missing all those 'staring out of the window times' years ago. The excellent teacher came out with the adage 'Remember-greed is the enemy'. 'Sell when you have made a profit and are satisfied and always leave something for the next man.' Wise words indeed. I built quite a portfolio for the next ten years of all new privatisation shares and as many know, it was practically impossible to go wrong if you remembered the basics of buying and selling. So thanks Mrs Thatcher and team for that sharing of the nation's wealth with me and buying our bungalow quicker than I thought possible. I did go wrong on one occasion when I listened to advice (the only time) from a work colleague and had a modest punt into a newly launched hi tech company-it went bust within a year and took my contribution with it.

Money-the having or lack of in my life has never been a strong focus. In early years I read of the idiot sons of the gentry who squandered vast sums on the gaming tables and of those who had achieved fame and fortune and then spiralled into a spending frenzy that never seemed to have contentment as the core objective. In my modest thinking of youth, I wanted a new motor-cycle which was just a dream never achieved-but a few years later a new car or an expensive Rolex watch for example was never on the wish list. I have had probably ten new company cars and the interest and smell of newness soon wears off. They were very appreciated perks for private use as well, but still just necessary transport. Finding out the correct time? I could always stand at the front door as I did years ago at Nan's house in Heywood and ask somebody. A real objective in increasing mid life income was to pay the mortgage off before the due date. We were able to make this happen now with years to spare. I always remember going into the local NatWest Bank to cancel the monthly standing order for the mortgage thinking 'That's it – now we have arrived as real property owners and are in control of our destiny'

This also gave the opportunity spend more on holiday time together with cruises and weeks in Italy and Spain in summer, plus building a nest egg for the future as retirement approached. A self awarded bonus for just us this time. Past years and most enjoyable they were, of being able to pay for holidays for our growing up family-or for them to go on their own and we got a pleasure from being able to do that. I was still earning an above average salary and often an annual bonus, so why not share it.

A memorable trip to Toronto, Canada for son Richard and grandson Chris to watch the Maple Leafs play ice hockey and to see the tumbling Niagara Falls with them. All very enjoyable times that we loved to make happen. Not that anyone could accuse me of spending wildly on frivolous spur of the moment accessories. Serious decisions and careful research to buy an old fashioned thermos flask that takes hot coffee all round the world (we have actually got three of them and have the photo's to prove it). A modest initial outlay from the wealth fund accumulating and you can sip away in front of the Egyptian Pyramids at Giza, in Piazza San Marco in Venice or at the top of the CN tower in Toronto and observe others giving you strange looks. Think of the money saved to pay for the next holiday.

The early 1990's brought Jack Benson into my life. He was the Gazette country writer living in nearby Little Eccleston with his weekly column of ranging interests of whatever took his fancy. Would start off as a walk he was taking on the nearby Bowland Fells for instance and divert to a human life story with a poignant ending. He was described by a fellow journalist as 'a rambling preambler and a very lovely man to know' which fits him well. He was also a truly exceptional teacher and communicator and encouragement for me to start writing.

He started various creative writing classes around the Fylde and I was one of his early attendee's and regular pupils. He had an easy way of explaining the long descriptive experience of putting thoughts to paper and the gentle reminder of correct grammar to use. For many of us in the class the immaculate and acceptable composition of a sentence to Oxford dictionary standard did not come easy-myself very much included to this day. He also had a way of dealing with it on a one to one basis. He marked in red ink my story offering of birch and hazel trees that had been coppiced on the local M55 motorway embankment over the years and how as time went by on my regular drive home I noticed...I will stop there and break to his input. 'Now then young John, you keep slipping from the past to the present tense and back again'. 'This is a good tale, but don't make me work hard to understand you telling it" He had slipped a corrective adjective here and there and deleted a bit of blather as he called it and gave it me back to me. His closing words quietly said would be 'It won't pass muster as the best English, but it's you telling the story and that's more important for readers to know that'. He said he was entitled to call me young John as he was ten years older than me and used to drop a line in the post, or speak on the phone with the prompt 'How's the book going young John? You have got in you to write lad, so get on with it' He was also responsible for one of my first proxy story efforts of a tale that I had told him on the phone and I was proud to see it in his Country Talk column soon after. The retelling of when four year old grandson Chris was in the car with Mum and Dad a week earlier. Jacks column piece went like this:

It will soon be a year since we nursed our refugee kestrel back to health, then passed it on to the Kestrel Lady to be retrained for the wild. We often wondered how it fared and our wonderings were renewed when a friend phoned to tell us of a kestrel seen in that area by a couple out driving with their four year old son. It was hovering gracefully as kestrels do and the boy's father stopped the car for a better look. 'What's that' asked the lad. 'A kestrel' said his father. What is it?' 'A kestrel' the lad repeated and the parents smiled fondly. Then without warning the bird swooped to the ground and reappeared carrying a mouse in its talons. The parents were horrified. What had started as a harmless bit of bird watching had turned abruptly into a demonstration of nature at her most cruel. They glanced apprehensively at the boy as the bird flew off with the mouse flopping feebly beneath it. Lower lip trembling, he asked the inevitable question. 'Daddy, what is the kestrel doing with that poor mouse' Daddy was still pounding his brain for the right answer when the little lad straightened his shoulders, blinked back his tears and said, 'I know. He's teaching it to fly.' Jack Benson. Evening Gazette Saturday April 30th 1988.

He also marked me well, with one of my later short story efforts I saved titled 'Funny Turns' and for the two Jacks mentioned, here it is.

FUNNY TURNS

I sometimes think back, as you do, a couple of years ago to a difficult time when I was regularly visiting my 90 year old stepfather, in a care home. He had married again after my mother died and following a partial stroke, had to go into a nursing home. A few months later his wife died and he spent many hours alone. My several times a week visits became difficult to stimulate in terms of conversation and new topics. You learn to carefully phrase an enquiry of How are you?' and 'have you had any visitors then' because of the negatives that come back. Far better to go in with news, however trivial and try and chat about other than his obvious lonely state and that the clock of life is ticking away. Not easy -as many will know. It's difficult to generate a positive conversation especially when memories fade and a general air of resignation fills these nursing and care homes with a sort of despair of living. This was not particular to the way this home was run. It was no different I would suggest from many others, where twenty or so very lonely people would sit in the lounge waiting to die. They tend to lose their dignity I found and rudeness and intolerance to each other becomes evident. These homes around the country have been the focus of much comment in recent years and some sorry tales have been uncovered. Undoubtedly there are others that are well run with a caring staff, but it must be a thankless job. My stepfather died after a few months in the home, his demise hastened by a fall and a resultant hip operation. He had told me more than once that he was ready to go and I understood how he must have felt.

Thankfully there were the lighter moments. A sort of black comedy that hopefully kept us both going in often stilted conversations over the months. He was quite deaf and relied on lip reading and one to one conversations. I know he would have smiled at other times of my telling of this tale.

One afternoon I went to visit and saw that he was in the lounge with some six other residents, grouped in chairs around a young man in nurse uniform. It transpired that he was a trainee from a local physiotherapy practice. He was demonstrating, with the use of soft coloured balls, how to squeeze slowly with one in each hand and do slow arm movements back and forward. Clearly a programme designed to help muscle tone and the recovery process the patient might need.

His technique and demonstration were being viewed in solemn faced silence. I watched for a few moments, without being seen and went to have a chat with the staff.

Later I saw my stepfather alone in his room and asked him for once, if he had any visitors since I last called a couple of days earlier.

'No – I don't think so. I haven't seen anybody for ages.' A longer pause.

'There was a young chap earlier on. He was some sort of turn you know.'

'One of those juggler's – but I didn't reckon much to him.'

-John Featherstone (April 2007)

Chapter Ten

As the nineties arrived the motorcycle market sales had their usual roller coaster dip and the decision was made by Heron Suzuki to relinquish the Vespa franchise and effectively the Italians took over distribution control. Hello parent company Piaggio from Pontedera and the deal that took myself and the soon to retire Ernie Hendy as part of the transfer. By this time Ernie and I had already made a pioneering move in the industry by taking the new 50cc Sfera demonstrator scooter's from Piaggio around the UK in a trailer hitched to the back of the company car for dealers to try out. A resounding success establishing what was to be a new era for the Italians, who had up till then relied on the traditional gear change Vespa scooters. A warm welcome as ever from Tim and Rachel Wade of Miles Kingsport in Hull and Frank and Lesley Robinson at Fiveways Motorcycles in the city. All these family business people as many others round the North of England and Scotland like Glenn at JK Hirst in Bradford, Ray Dell in Pudsey, Dighton and Tim at Dyrons in Leeds who helped me when I needed it most. Too many to name, but thanks to all and even the very few who would not know a good turn if they fell over one!

One again I meet a special influence in life and this time it's a Sicilian called Giuseppe Tranchina who is charged with masterminding the new operation based in Orpington, Kent. The first meeting is less than tranquil with my new boss, as just before the signed deal between Heron and the Piaggio factory Ernie and I had been given the lucrative opportunity to sell some 800 in stock Vespa scooters from Heron into dealers at a very special price-with a perk bonus for ourselves of course. Opportunity Knocks for two street wise sales representatives. The telephone lines were ringing. We had perhaps 4 days to make it happen and we did. Every Vespa dealer in the country had extra stock scoots squeezed into sheds at home and that year's Mediterranean cruise was taken care of. Fast forward to the sell in business plan for the next few months of newcomer to the market place Giuseppe and the closed doors reception he got from stuffed up dealers.! He was not pleased. But we got over that and the good times were coming back again and the commuter market sales for go to work machines did improve.

GT as he was easier known, recruited Shirley Pattison for marketing and PR to help him put Piaggio and Vespa back where it belonged at the top of the sales charts. Sales incentive trips for dealers and wives and partners and all staff to Rome, Florence and the Greek Islands became the must do, with no expense spared. Typical would have been a visit from me to see Paul and Val Hamilton at Motech Scooters in Newcastle on Tyne. 'Paul, you have to buy six of these new 125 scoots called the ET4 and you and Val get a trip to Rome'

Cautious and thoughtful Paul would have said 'Hang on a minute John, I need to think about this' A small pause and a voice from the real boss at the back who said. 'Write them down-we are going' from Val who to this day is remembered with love by all who knew her. With their close friends Graham and Sue Best from Kegra Scooters in Southend, that is just one of the many tales we tell of the nineties to this day. Booming years when close dealer working relationships and economic conditions with Euro free legislation, helped to make working in the two wheel market place profitable and enjoyable.

No little thanks to GT and later Massimo Mirosi and some very supportive thinking from the long experienced Italian factory. Once again I meet up with others from far and wide who remain to this day as good friends and always there to tell the truth. Pete from Fowlers, Mike 'laughing boy' Busher and not forgetting Mark Franklin and Simone Niccolai who have been all round the world helping the Italians to succeed bless them. Mark from London who I had a head to head rivalry with, as we each competed to be the best at increasing sales and market share in a traditional North v South rivalry.

Simone (another Mr Nice Guy) who I introduced to England on visits to see the network around the UK when he arrived from Italy. Never to forget a special visit when Jan and I were invited to his parents home for dinner in Casci di Buti (superb) and then his wedding to Carlotta when we were the only English guests. A memorable occasion. Time for another true story of opportunity and good fortune. In fact all my stories are true, if perhaps a slight embellishment here and there.

Once again it's the annual NEC show in Birmingham and this time Piaggio have a bigger than ever stand presence after many years of growing sales and we are seriously threatening Honda with being number one in the market. Being senior staff CEO by now and a very sober fellow to boot, I am elected the stand manager by Massimo Mirosi, the new country manager and responsible for the smooth running over the ten day period of the Piaggio display and customer hospitality. We always had plenty of drink on the stand for trade days especially and this time to really push 'the bike' out, we have TV chef Antonio Carluccio's team from London to serve authentic Italian food. Pride of place is a gigantic Parmigiano Reggiano wheel of the best Italian Parmesan cheese valued around £450 at the time. Original weight of a full wheel is some 38kg (84lb). The top crust is thinly sliced off and tiny spoons provided for tasty scoops. It went down well on a very busy first trade day served with a range of excellent Italian specialities. Second trade day was similar and the order books bursting with massive forward orders. The end of a long big order day and the prospect for all staff on the stand of a welcome visit to the hotel bar to celebrate – but not for me, as I cleared away and checked all was in order for the next busy public day opening.

The next question I had prepared for exactly the right moment to put to Massimo as he and I prepared to leave the stand last. 'This wheel of cheese Massimo-it's open at the top and not going to improve being left out is it? Do you want me to take care of it' A knowing look in my direction and a dismissive wave of his hand. 'Take it home' he said. Nothing more to do then except spend the next hour or so carrying the by now nibbled, but still 70lb or so of cheese in my arms, across a wet and cold deserted NEC car park to the boot of my car parked half a mile away. Frequent stops with rasping breath, sweating like mad and aching arms wrapped around my prize bonus, but the absolute satisfaction of another daft idea achieved.

It was ceremoniously sliced into around 2lb wedges and into the freezer back at home and lasted for some four years I recall. One of the lads next day on the stand recovering from the previous night foray to the hotel celebration bar said 'Hey Feathers– where's that cheese gone. I was going to nick some of that to take home'. I said 'Must have gone to a needy family Jason who were a bit quicker off the mark than you'. The hesitation is with me to this day at paying out a couple of quid for a tiny sliver of Parmesan to grate over the pasta. Must be those early wonderful mind forming days of frugal living that keeps me thinking carefully of values. My granddaughter Amy was born in 1996 and I am pleased to have been a large part of her growing up years and I love her very much. I have to say that, because when I struggle to move computer files around or try and get things right with my limited knowledge of word document she is on hand to encourage and put right my mistakes.

Which got me to thinking that with some, conversation is difficult and others can literally go 'rabbiting on forever' as the saying goes. But there is no more enjoyable times I have found than the early years of conversations with children free of inhibition and full of sweet innocence. They speak from the heart and feelings of the moment when the first sentences are put together. Quite literally 'out of the minds of babes and innocents come…' some of the best entertainment and thought provoking lines. I found that the knack is to treat them not as children but to try and strike a bond of equality and interest. Their tiny minds already have been battered with 'Oh, isn't she growing into a lovely little girl' by adoring Auntie perhaps and 'He certainly looks more like his Daddy since we last saw him' all said with smiling stares of approval as though they were fashion accessories. A little over powering perhaps for the recipient of this praise as they shuffle feet and look away. Then the standard inquisition of 'and which class are you in-have you got many new friends and who is your teacher?'-and the party stopper of 'I went to your school' and other mind blowing standard offerings. Result is often the head down silent reaction that can't cope with all this. That's not for me. Always aware that you speak first only when Mum and Dad are present, my golden rule is to elevate their age up a few years and try and communicate as though they are adult. Does not always work, but a day out a few years ago gave Jan and I a memory to always look back on as very special indeed.

We had decided early on a promising summer day to have a drive up the motorway and have a walk around Hutton in the Forest which is a small stately home with forested grounds near Penrith in Cumbria. Very few cars there when we arrived mid morning and onto the parking area we went and noticed that a family of Dad and Mum with two young boys around probably four and seven were organising change of footwear to set off for a walk. Calmly standing around with slow waving tail was Henry, the golden retriever that most relaxed and pleasant breed of dogs. Now that name is the only one we remember of the family, but we were told that they had come for a forest walk to burn the energy off two excitable young men. Turned out the parents were teachers at Sedbergh School, a preparatory and boarding school near to Kendal and not as far down the M6 as we had travelled that morning. Well one was excitable and voluble.

Older brother who was immediately not lost for a word or more, confidently said of his brother 'He's not five yet and can't talk as much as me and we're going exploring into the woods soon' So that was it for starters and off we trooped first into the network of forest paths. I had a feeling a challenge was coming on. We were some hundred yards ahead of the family group and quietly strolling along, but well aware of the from time to time of rushing about in undergrowth and shout's from behind. We came to an unmarked split in the path and by now thicker undergrowth in this well established forest. We stopped to decide which way and were soon joined by expedition leader and his assistant. Mum and Dad were within hearing when I tried my first line. 'Excuse me young man. Can you help us please? We think we are lost and not sure which path to go on, especially if we meet some wild animals or perhaps gorilla's swinging about in the trees.' And that started it. We were immediately taken into care and under his leadership pointed to the main route. I asked about some small rodent holes in the path, what they were and if they could find a big stick for us, as we might have to fight our way through the jungle ahead. We sort of carried on together with me insisting the two brothers went a couple of yards ahead, as I could easily get frightened. Just the responsibility they needed. By this time confidence is growing and youngest finds a newly dug rabbit hole and rushes over to put his hand in mine and pull me over and show me. A lovely walk was had and a word or two with amused parents as we came out into the open area near the lake. Elder boy went to his Mum and apparently said 'Is that man and lady coming with us' and was not pleased apparently, when told we might be tired so they had to go on without us. We went on our way and had a picnic lunch in the grounds, with what else but the trusty thermos flasks. We were going back to the car park later in the afternoon when we saw the family about to leave. Mum came over to us and said 'I have to tell you what that youngest son of mine has just said to me' Word for word. 'Mummy, you know that man over there we saw and made adventures with. I think I have fallen in love with him'

An absolutely special moment, that brought a tear to my eye.

Chapter Eleven

All was going well in life and my work was fine after some quite busy years, but the annual hefty mileage now starting to be a problem. Not just that the staying away from home that was always on the agenda most weeks, but made easier when Jan was able to come with me for the overnight stays. She had retired now from her part time job she enjoyed so much. She worked for Mr and Mrs Edsforth who owned a chemist's shop on Highfield Road. Not quite the Saturday girl as she used to say, but was always a pleasure to work for them in a traditional courteous working pharmacy with many a customer tale to tell. Good times to finish her working career with appreciation on both sides. Her proud boast is that she travelled with me to most towns in the North and Scotland over the years. The days when you could be dropped off in a town centre near every Marks & Spencer she knew the exact location of. I went on dealer calls and would pick her up at say 5pm at a bus stop in Dundee near the shopping area and then on to the hotel in Blairgowrie perhaps. No problem with traffic and no need for a mobile phone to text 'where are you?'-Not that she has a mobile phone to this day and seems to survive quite well without. It worked, but we would hesitate to make any shopping arrangements like that now.

Still there was something else that I wanted to achieve as the age of sixty approached. We still did quite bit of walking over the years. Nothing too taxing for most of the time, but I had picked up again on reading Alfred Wainwright's books after a broken ankle enforced rest at home, following a Langdales route trek with son Stephen in the Lake District hills. AW was the one who devised the Coast to Coast walk from St Bees in Cumbria with a scenic 192 mile meandering route avoiding civilisation in the main, to Robin Hood's Bay in Yorkshire. His quote leapt out at me that 'ambition in life should be an objective or life does indeed… become an aimless wandering.' Well-I had done a bit of wandering, so the 'objective' has to be made to happen. Time now to go the story notes I wrote up during my walk in April 1998 and finally put together some months later.

AW TOLD FIBS…
Coast to Coast, in the footsteps of
Alfred Wainwright – April 1998

A twelve day walk from St Bees in Cumbria to Robin Hood's Bay in Yorkshire in April 1998. One hundred and ninety two miles of sun, rain, pain and the sheer joy of achievement.

* * * * * * * *

'The inside of the turned back greyish bed sheets held no welcome for my aching body. I stood fully clothed in dripping waterproofs, by the side of the iron framed bed in the dingy room having found a new use for my walking pole with the warm musty room smell mingled with my own sweaty odour. A further flick of the pole turned the sheets back under the faded pink candlewick spread. Droplets of rain still hanging from my face and clothing I stood and felt at my lowest ebb.'

Five days out and sixty miles on with one hundred and thirty to go. I had just the energy to hang my backpack and boots behind the door. Still with waterproof jacket and over trousers on, I laid down and drifted off into a less than fitful sleep.

Welcome to my squalid room above the village pub. The stair rod rain still hammered down outside on the deserted street. Through the yellowish torn net curtain the neon strip light around a pub sign, glowed dimly in the best of American b movie tradition.

Like many others before me I started with some admiration of Alfred Wainwright. This undoubtedly talented writer and illustrator, whose idea it was in the early 1970's to map out a footpath route that roughly went, as the crow flies, across the roof of England from the Irish Sea to the North Sea.

I started off by copying his pen and ink drawings of mountains, dry stone walls and buildings from the many illustrations in his books of Lakeland walks. I do not profess to have any particular skill in this direction but the interest came when I was plaster bound for several weeks as the result of a broken ankle. The enforced rest gave me a most relaxing time sitting with a small cartridge paper book and various grade ink pens faithfully copying at first and then creating my own pastoral and Lakeland village scene. The idea that I would attempt the 'Coast to Coast' did not arrive with me overnight. I reckon though that something like this was always on the cards. I was fifty five years old at the time and for a six footer about a stone overweight at thirteen something. I was also at life's reflective point where the word retirement comes up on the discussion agenda with more frequency. It's also a time to look back perhaps and think what you have achieved and in my case certainly in a sporting or physical achievement sense, my trophy room lies bare.

At grammar school you were forced on many wet and cold afternoons to run up and down a field clutching a lump of odd shaped leather whilst so called friends tried to kick your legs from under you. Cross country running held memories of pain wracked lungs and sodden black pumps. Bunter shapes alongside weedy, youthful bodies were all exhorted to 'get a move on and act like men' This held no appeal for me and the years passed without my sampling other than a country stroll here and there. That's really how the idea came about on one of my muses down Memory Lane.

If I was going to achieve anything of note for my own personal satisfaction, then what better than to go for a walk ...a bit longer than usual.

* * * * * * * *

AW does indeed tell fibs... his account of the walk talks of majestic views across Lakeland and the North Yorkshire Moors. His simple descriptions are of nature and landscapes at their best(which is true). If only you could see them.

He makes the 192 miles seem like a series of Sunday afternoon strolls and goes out of his way to play down the thousands of feet of ascent and descent of mountain and moorland. It is not so much a walk as an endurance test with mile after mile of boggy stretches and flinty paths on a roller coaster traverse. Foot slogging pain is the norm.

The obligatory Lakeland mist at 1,000 feet swirls around the Coaster tempting him to detour in circles and exceed his daily quota of miles. The inevitable horizontal rain and tugging wind conspire to annoy and detract from pleasure. The rucksack increases in weight daily without addition and leg and back pain are matched by thoughts of packing it all in. 'What am I doing here?' You can curse him openly. He is not listening and neither is anyone else. All this is strangely forgotten as the day's progress till finally you walk down to the harbour at Robin Hood's Bay on the North Sea and AW is forgiven. The sheer joy of achievement takes over.

My preparations started in January 1998. I obtained O.S strip maps and guide and accommodation books from the Town Hall at Kendal, to supplement the excellent video that AW had recorded with the writer Eric Robson.

In this he retraced many of the sections and comes up with the conclusion that it is ideally staged to take twelve days walking. I took the advice. I also worked out that April would be an ideal month... not too warm and the drying spring sun and longer days would give me little rain. Wrong. It was one of the wettest Aprils for many years. Clothing and rucksack to be attended to. A visit to the specialist shops of Anorak City (as the locals supposedly call Ambleside) fitted me up with full set of proofed jacket and trousers. Boots and rucksack were chosen with equal care as was the invaluable walking pole. For the first time in many years I looked at the price ticket last.

You can opt for bed and breakfast or camping. You can also have your luggage transported to each overnight stop. I went for the semi macho route of accommodation at night with pack on my back. This entailed some planning with overnight bed and breakfast, to be booked with some difficulty. Turned out to be other than myself with the idea of walking the Coast to Coast in April. In the most remote area of Keld at halfway there are certainly more sheep than people but I managed it and deposits duly sent off. An early decision was to do the trek on my own. My wife Jan was not enamoured with the same zeal, but nonetheless was my encouragement every step of the way and my "voice and soul" when I needed it most. Scorn, ridicule, support and puzzlement had been poured on me in the preceding weeks by some of my best friends and family. Typical of the encouragement was:

'Got to admire you – wish I felt I was up to it.'

'All the best pal-I know you will make it.'

'Have a great time and don't forget to post the cards on the way.'

Others settled for: 'Have you got a mental problem and need to find yourself?'

'So that's it then – do you want picking up after the first day – or the first 100 yards – ho ho ho. Don't make me laugh – what, in your state.'

Training consisted of a few short evening walks around home town St Annes the week before and to get used to the new boots. Methylated spirit was dabbed on the soles of my feet – it seemed the thing to do.

DAY ONE – SUNDAY 18th APRIL 1998

Son and daughter in law took me the eighty mile journey from home to the start line at St Bees. A salty tang of Irish Sea air came on the light westerly breeze in the blue cloud scudded sky. A perfect day to start a walk.

'So see you at Robin Hood's-and don't break your other leg' was the parting shot from my loved ones referring to a Switzerland walk mishap. I did the suggested dipping of boots in the lapping waves on the sandy shore and headed past a small sign that simply said 'Start C to C.'

No fanfare –just a wave back from the ascended cliff top and I was away with very mixed emotions. It was eleven in the morning and destination was a hotel at Ennerdale Bridge fourteen miles away. Now take it easy-it's not a race. If I could average my usual pace of two and a half miles an hour then no problem. The roller coaster cliff top path took me easily along then inland to the village of Cleator for first planned stop for butties and flask in solidly packed rucksack. Only the first stop was quicker and revealed first mistake. I was sweating like mad with fleece layer under waterproof jacket. Offending fleece spent the rest of the day tied onto the rucksack.

N.B Fleece and spare boots were abandoned at Grasmere at the end of day three for collection later.

Cricket match was in progress at Cleator in mid-afternoon and food and drink was taken ringside. In fact I ate all I had with me including three days planned chocolate supply. Second mistake and lesson for every day afterwards. Only ever snack eat during the walk. Laid back in the warm sunshine listening to that very English slap of leather on willow and thought. 'This is going to be a doddle.' Suppose I should get going. Eight miles on the clock and feeling, well, quite full actually. If the route book is right that hill in the distance should be Dent at 1,000 feet above sea level. Stirred out of lethargy and yes, legs did feel a bit stiff and phew -shouldn't have eaten all that. I made it to the hilltop at a very slow dragging pace. With glances at the map I cut into the forestry plantation for easy enough walking on forestry roads. Occasional birdsong and met not a soul. A couple of miles went by and I seemed to be in the wood longer than…hang on why is that beautiful sunset I see through the trees facing me? OK perhaps the sun sets in the East in Cumbria – time for a proper look at the route this time. Cutting the story short, I did manage to get out of the wood eventually – struggle over a boggy moor and rejoin the road into Ennerdale. Enough lessons I think for one day.

Trudged into the hotel early evening with just enough interest to look in the failing light and pick out Pillar and the mountains of Lakeland that await me. Been alone all day – quite a strange feeling. I had sought this solitude but wanted to tell someone how I felt yet not seek company. Time to phone home.

DAY TWO

The stillness and sweetness of a quiet village and I was on my way with aching legs for the first easy mile by road to the lake shore. The walking pole(already proving a valuable asset) taps me on my way like Blind Pew looking for Jim Hawkins. Yellow clumps of gorse dot the fields around with early white and pink thorn flowers in the hedgerows. A good to be alive morning. Met up with a couple I had seen at breakfast and exchanged a greeting. They are of a similar age and on the same mission as myself. That's what happened over the journey – fellow coasters walked together for a while and perhaps saw each other again the next day having gone to different booked accommodation. For the most part the aimed for solitude was my companion. It gave me a very few down moments and when this happened the phone call back home to straighten me out was the tonic needed.

At Ennerdale Water this beautiful spring morning the route was easy to follow with another fourteen mile section today. Follow the right shore to the end of the lake and the forestry road through to the most remote of the YHA hostels-the Black Sail Hut.

The location of this bunkhouse is simply stunning with views on all sides of the best that the Lake District can offer. If you ever get the chance to visit this remote valley then please do. You will be rewarded with the ultimate river and bridge setting where the crystal clear gurgling River Ehen courses over the most delicate light green slate. A joy to stand and stare. No created for television garden water feature could ever get near to what nature can provide in simplistic beauty.

Twenty three miles from journey start to here and the first real test. Destination is Rosthwaite in Borrowdale and to get there you have to climb some 1,500feet alongside tumbling Loft Beck towards Brandreth and Honister. This is the first fib encountered in the AW descriptions I had pored over in the winter months. He refers to rising ground and the 'pull by Loft Beck' and the awaited 'spanking walkers route of Moses Trod.' The reality was a little different. Again late in the day I clawed my way up this vertical hillside with gasping breath and glanced upwards with despairing eyes to the bank of mist. I relied on grabbing at tussocks of grass and slate slabs to drag upwards with pack back seeming to double its weight.

I got there and into the swirling mist. Panic is not the word – just a little unease. I had never used a compass in my life – reckoned that if I was properly equipped and stuck to the paths. All you have to do is stay on the paths I you can see them…If I had once again just read the route and map a little slower, rather than the glance and gone more to the right than the path straight ahead. So it was down towards the Honister mine workings instead of keeping my height gained. I finally had the sense to swing right and pick up the old tramway track and on down to Rosthwaite and second day journey's end. The last couple of road miles brought the sound of rhythmic marching feet behind me.

'Alright then?' was the greeting.

Three commando style attired specimens came along-side. Each was carrying a shed on his back with poles sticking out. Lightweight waterproof jackets and track-suit bottoms hugged these perfect bodies and clearly they were on a mission.

'We want to crack on and see how quick we can do it.'

'Oh right' I said 'Good luck – won't keep you-guess you will probably be having a pint at Robin Hood's Bay whilst I'm still struggling to reach half way.'

Three days later I found out that they had packed it in at Patterdale.

That was a story repeated over the next few days. The younger starters tended to have a drop out rate

higher than the 'plodding oldies.' What helped get me
through was an inherent stubborn attitude to make it.
Realistically, I was not going to do this sort of thing
again, so why make all the effort in vain. Not a death
wish – just a desire confided by others. Another day and
the rain was coming down in a very Lakeland way in
Borrowdale.

DAY THREE
On familiar ground for the next two days which took
me over Greenup Edge at 2,000 feet, along a switch-
back ridge walk from Calf Crag to Helm Crag – then
the descent into the Easedale valley and Grasmere
for the night. Left the hotel soon after eight and enjoyed
the watery sunshine for the next hour or so as the
ribbon track climbed out of Borrowdale. The damp
smell pervaded as the mist thickened. Eagle Crag
alongside Stonethwaite Beck is a towering profile as
you pass by and the eerie stillness is broken only by the
slide of water on slate. The trademark mist continued
for most of the day and goes a long way to dispelling
the myth that the Lake District actually has views.
Afternoon and my first planned meet up with family
went well. Younger son Stephen had travelled from
home that morning and time arranged was 3pm at the
top of Helm Crag. He was ten minutes late. He journe-
yed with me for the next two days and had to slow
his pace to suit mine.

The B and B in Grasmere that night proved an excellent choice with instant offer of drying room for boots
and for practically the whole of the sodden inside
of rucksack. All shirts and underwear were sporting
rainbow colours. I could not care less.!

DAYS FOUR & FIVE

Took us the long ascent over Grisedale to the bottom of Dollywagon Pike and the gloomy Grisedale Tarn. Again some 2,000 feet up in the mist and the choice is given to continue the long meandering route into Patterdale valley or strike upwards for the Helvellyn range and the traverse of the infamous Striding Edge. No contest today. It's the lower one for us though we have done the Edge in less than ideal conditions. A reminder once again is given in AW's notes and to be fair he does say:

'This is a fine moment with the tarn immediately below and the unremitting wall of Dollywagon Pike dispelling many a notion of a detour over Helvellyn. Eminently more inviting is the noble profile of St Sunday Crag beyond the tarns outflow, and if considering an alternative route to Patterdale, this presents the easier option.' O.K – sort of correct up to a point but he doesn't really make it clear that the St Sunday route on the other side of the valley is a ribbon track on a razored edge reaching up into the sky and today disappearing into the mist. Tonight it's a pub to stay in -that's alright but the compact rooms are above the bar and when somebody down below is absolutely killing themselves with laughter in the early hours...

More winding into the mist and rain next day and the final range to cross before saying goodbye to the Lake District at Shap. It was farewell to son on mist shrouded Kidsty Pike as he then made his way back west. That's the one, if ever you are travelling north on the M6 on clear days only, you can glance across and see a tilted pyramid some six miles away. Down along-side Haweswater from Riggindale and the last tramp of the day in driving rain to Shap village.

You have to picture the next scene. I am cold, tired of course and hungry. Just a bit depressed and not helped by rain and sweat dripping off my Vaseline smeared nose for most of the day and mingled with wet tissue and soggy gloves is exacerbating the developing cold sores around my mouth. Quite severe aching legs and back. This is the nearest point to home and I am tempted. The premature gloom of evening takes me along the main street with swishing water from passing trucks and cars giving my boots a colour change. Tapping along with curved back I arrive at tonight's choice. The faded exterior holds no promise and to this day I see the grey net curtains masking the scene within. A dark interior with flashing Bally gaming machine and figure perched on bar stool. It is indeed a pub/hotel or whatever and my chosen abode for the night.

Door is unbolted and slurred voice confirms I am expected. Good sense says turn away and go and lie down in a bus shelter or start knocking on other doors for a bed.

Some madness, or the interests of research allows me to be shown up to a squalid room. A TV set of early origin held together with ducting tape is the main accessory. A cracked washstand and crazed mirror completes the scene. Mine host indicates, in measured tones, that I could choose from any of three rooms available. This one narrowly won. I stand in the centre of this dump and for the first time in years feel that I may be near to tears of anger. How did I come to end up here for the night?

The inside of the turned-back grey sheets held no welcome for my aching body. I stood fully clothed by the side of the iron framed bed having found a new use for my walking pole. The warm musty room mingled with my own sweaty state as I flick the turned sheets back under the faded pink candlewick spread. Droplets of rain still hanging from face and clothing I feel at my lowest ebb. Five days out with sixty miles on and one hundred and thirty to go – just had the energy to hang my backpack and boots behind the door. Still with waterproof jacket and over trousers on I laid down and drifted off into a less than fitful sleep. The stair rod rain outside still hammered down on the deserted street. Through the torn net yellowing curtain the neon strip light glows dimly in the best of American b movie traditions...

DAYS SIX & SEVEN
Morning at last and away over the limestone pavements through to Kirkby Stephen and the Pennines into Yorkshire on day six. Mixed feelings but the determination remains...just. The inside map pocket zipper was kept busy as always for that essential double check when you start to relax and the mind wanders.

Excellent welcoming guest house in KS on the High Street (with initials the same as mine) in this busy market town, took me in search of the Nine Standards the next morning for day seven. Stone landmarks of uncertain origin mark the watershed – rainfall to the west is destined for the Irish Sea and to the east, Swaledale and ultimately the North Sea.

Various stories abound of the origin of these standing stones – to give the impression of a camped army to repel invaders perhaps? But no Goretex, GPS equipment or polyamide mesh linings for these soldiers of old. Wet leather sandals would have been the army issue for all seasons.

A fine viewpoint which I admired before the horizontal rain appeared again and stayed with me for four hours as I sloshed across the boggiest moor so far to Keld. The bog patches to be avoided are the smooth ones close to reed grass. Slightly crusted they mask an interior of treacly black brown liquid that sucks and clings to boot and legs. My grandmother would have called it slutch.

I counted ten stone dwellings before reaching mine for the night in the village of Keld. A farm I passed in the gathering gloom as the torrents of water from Whitsundale Beck raged by I discovered later was called Ravenseat.

This trudge past in lashing rain was to later be a very decisive trigger in my memory recall of life and finally writing this book. Inside the farmhouse that day would have been Clive and Amanda Owen and she later wrote an excellent book of life at Ravenseat called 'The Yorkshire Shepherdess' More of that sequence of events later.

Halfway at ninety five miles and no going back. Bit of self satisfaction has to creep in. You need something positive to focus on to go through those quiet hours you spend alone to keep the spirits up. I found it so easy to go from one emotion of elation, to feeling why am I doing this and into a down feeling all within a short space of time and not really knowing why. Tell yourself that others would not have made it so far. Picture the map of England and you are the tiny dot halfway across. The feeling wears off as stubborn determination returns.

DAY EIGHT

I opted for the longest stage so far with over twenty miles to Richmond. The route is simple. By and large follow the Swale river valley downwards. I did it but the last few miles seemed for ever. Varied terrain past the wonderfully named Old Gang Smelt Mill and Surrender Bridge evoking memories of the industrial past and then the villages of Reeth and Grinton. Twenty two miles to be exact and the last tarmac mile into town was like stepping on hot coals.

If you live in Richmond I suppose you get used to the church bell in the square that strike the hour through the night. Not sure if I heard five chimes-every other set I counted up till then-and finally gave up and climbed from a less than good night's sleep at six chimes. The thought of another days walk....felt very down for a while.

DAY NINE

The end coming up now so the feeling that I was sort of getting there had to help. I worked on that repetitive thought ... Weather improving and determination still had the edge over pain. I was eating well every night and morning but sensed that exercise was burning off any possible weight gain and even with a care free diet I still lost half a stone over the trip. Day nine(another long stage with easy walking) took me across the Vale of Mowbray to destination for the night at Ingleby Cross. By this time I had taken several photographs of varied subject matter. Perhaps it was the side effects of the daily painkillers and the solitude but my favourites remain of C. to C. direction signs with my trusty companions of rucksack and walking pole adorning same.

Another is of a lonely field when, with the sudden onset of a driving rainstorm, I was surrounded by a herd of steaming cows seeking shelter like myself under the trees.

Funny thing was they had weighed up the situation quicker than me and were already heading for cover whilst I was still looking at the rapidly darkening sky. It's inconsequential thoughts and events such as these, that I found such a welcome diversion to my idling mind.

That evening I had a very pleasant stone built house all to myself. Full of antiques and lovingly collected items over the years by the owner who lived next door. A gem of a B and B and a welcome recharge for batteries needed to ascend the Yorkshire Moors.

DAY TEN

The next day trek followed for many miles the Lyke Wake walk, through banks of heather that must be a blaze of colour in July and August. To keep you on your toes after the lovely valley of Scugdale is the big dipper traverse of Carlton Moor, Cringle Moor and Hasty Bank. No problem with the views that afternoon and I had looked down many miles to industrial Cleveland – studded here and there with farm fields sporting yellow patches of oil seed plants. The other unwelcome view was of was of the next ascent and descent when I was still labouring up the first one.

I had one more surprise overnight stop. I had booked a bed for the night a few miles off the route. It was a remote farm and the arrangement was to collect me by car when I reached a pub at a moorland road crossing.

I had visions of Aga cooker with massive breakfast and friendly family making this weary soul comfortable for the night. Not quite. Sturdy lady in Lada saloon with hay and straw replacing most of the back seat collected me at the pub. I stepped back in time over the next few hours to a rather damp and character smelling abode in Farndale. It was a livestock farm with husband and wife having some sort of living.

That was within minutes of us bouncing up the track into the farmyard. They reckon that some of these farmer types never throw anything away and this was one of them. The yard was littered with a rotting Ferguson tractor and implements from centuries past. I thought back later of these two when the devastation of foot and mouth arrived and wondered how they coped...

DAY ELEVEN

I'm nearly into single figures in miles to go now and end up spending the last evening having passed a signpost saying Whitby and Robin Hood's Bay. A very nice guest house was just what I needed at Hawsker to give myself a nice sort of stroll to the finish line and it was. Peaceful and quiet and I slept with a quiet sense of a hopefully forthcoming achievement ...made it at last and nearly there !

DAY TWELVE – THE LAST ONE

And it was the best weather so far. A truly superb spring morning with my first sight of the North Sea as I rounded a bend going out of the village lane south east. Brought just a catch to my throat and a moistening of the eyes and I felt a pride and quiet satisfaction that the end was in sight. Happy in mind and weak in body I looked forward to planned family meet on the cliff top. A couple walking towards me stopped for a chat and said:

'Have you come far then' with wonderful timing and genuine enquiry.

'Er, well yes. I've just walked across England' was the reply in less than steady voice. I allowed myself that bit of immodesty. Mobile phones have their uses, even if they only work mainly on the tops of mountains. But this morning it had worked when it was most needed to arrange our family reunion.

It was early afternoon as I walked the cliff top path from Hawsker with first sight of the finish line down below in the rocky strewn cove. The sun was out and warm on my face and the gentle breeze off the land flattening the lead blue sea. With jacket tied around my middle, I saw a family group some way off heading towards me. We could not have contrived a more fitting time and place. Even the gulls overhead sensed the occasion and lent their clamour to the happy moment, with tears and group hugs all round. Leg pain went for the last mile down to the harbour.

The photographs – the second dipping this time in the North Sea of my new best friends, my trusty totally waterproof boots that served me so well. A few minutes to take it all in and experience a very strange calming feeling inside.

I had made it !I have a simple indulgence certificate number 5488 from the Bay Hotel that says I completed the one hundred and ninety two mile Coast to Coast walk in twelve days on the 29th April 1998.

John Featherstone

G.T. who put Piaggio on the map in the UK

Massimo Mirosi

Wearing these glasses he always had
problems adding up my commission.

Mark, Me,
Jason & Mike.

Would you buy a bike from this lot?

With 'Mr Vespa'
Ernie Hendy.

In Rome for launch of ET4 Piaggio In 1996.

With Paul Smith at Expo Show 2016.

(From left) With Michael, Ed & Steve at Expo.

The 'A' Team at Piaggio.

(Left to right) Mark, Steve, Mike, Jason, Me & Paul at NEC Show, Piaggio Sales Force 2001.

Start of Coast to Coast Walk, 18th April 1998.

190 Miles, 12 Days.

Half way, onwards to Kirkby Stephen...

Helvellyn in winter.

Stephen & I on
Helvellyn in summer.

Lunch break on Helvellyn.

Jan & I in Robin Hood's Bay.

Family meet-up in Robin Hood's Bay, 1998.

Two miles to the end of Coast to Coast Walk, 1998.

Chapter Twelve

The achievement factor did not sit with me too long on the return home after the walk. But it did leave me with quite a lot of reflective thinking time as spring moved into summer and another birthday. Not that I felt very old or much different. My weight remained around 13 stone as it had done for some ten years or so and I always the made the slight effort from time to time to lose a few pounds, but nothing serious. Health fairly good with inevitable aches and pains after long car journeys but always tried to avoid going seeing my local GP. On a rare visit to him, Dr Thorpe who being the man of direct approach he is, said something like 'you must be one of the fittest on my books' which I took as a dismissal and compliment and a mental note to continue to avoid seeing him if possible.

Most of all that summer became a time to look back and think what else there was that could occupy my time and one answer was to write more. Jack Benson was about to give up reminding me, so as an interim to the book of life the short stories and motorcycle trade magazine letters became a focus. Over the many years making observations of motorcycle distribution and retailing I have come up with some recurring thoughts. Could be applied to lots of circumstances I reckon but always hard to find a single determining factor when the things that are going well become the downhill slope. First conclusion is the similarity to my own life of a roller coaster that goes in peaks and troughs. You always try to carry on towards the peak as human nature and enthusiasm takes you there, but often cannot do other than cope with the slide down. Bit like starting pushing treacle uphill. Others may find it easier to bury a head in the sand, as they do not have the emotional ability to cope-and for those people who cannot do anything about this feeling it must be a terrible burden. A soul so afraid of dying or trying, they never learned to live.

There was another spur around this time to lead me once again to the typing keys and communicate thought's that had been with me for years. First perhaps too direct a title of yet another short story offering could be Love, Friendship and True feelings are for every day – not just for Christmas.' But that was a bit direct and been used before to mention dogs. So I settled for a message to friends and family that did not exactly get rave reviews. Saying that the opinions from a few I did value said afterwards well done for standing up and being counted. The silent ones probably thought I was losing the plot and blamed my increasing age or perhaps thought my comments irrelevant. Matter of choice.

So here it is. Christmas greetings of a sort in 2004...

CHRISTMAS GREETINGS
An open letter to family and
friends – Remembrance Sunday, 14th Nov 2004

The first couple of attempts to write this have ended up in the recycle bin.

Sometimes the best thoughts are those that you put to paper and then rewrite over the next day or so to allow your true feelings to show through...

Indeed, early draft offerings met with 'you can't say that' from my in house editor and arbiter of tact and management. So what am I on about?

The obligatory pointless exercise of giving and receiving mostly unwanted presents in a society that materially has more than it can cope with... the only thing it may lack is the time, love and thought for others that made up the original concept of Christmas.

More than ever in recent years the sheer commercialism and drift away from what, after all, is a religious festival makes the so called celebrations an excuse for excess, that I do not need to form part of my life.

The traditional pleasure of giving and receiving has been taken away in our over supplied material society. Those most vulnerable to this are the children who could only think of asking for money for phone credits when asked what gift they would wish for. Isn't it farcical that we have come to this. Is it wrong to make a stand against this sorry state of affairs for fear of causing offence with family and friends, or be accused of having a 'funny turn.' Gifts of goods or money should not be conditional and yet I would not want to contribute any of my money, mostly earned over 45 years of working, to some object that is not wanted or needed or worse still discarded early in the New Year.

We would not wish to receive any presents this year... or realistically any more at all. We have, like most, everything we need and if any further good fortune comes our way we would like it to be from an outside source, such as Premium Bonds.

Better rein in there or it will start to sound like 'binned version one.'

Last night we went to a Salvation Army brass band concert... a first for us. We are not regular churchgoers as you know, or have any particular strong religious beliefs. It was just a thought provoking evening out though, with obligatory but very enjoyable singing of Jerusalem and Land of Hope and Glory to finish off. What I do remember was a particularly moving address, asking for financial support for a new building, from the director of Bryan House – a local hospice for children. I didn't need an excuse to know how to be satisfied with my rewards in life and pass it on in another direction. It was a timely reminder to convince me what to do this Christmas and the disquiet I feel over present giving and receiving.

This comes as a typed version and no apology needed if you remember my handwriting. I sincerely hope it conveys how I feel. Christmas cards can have a purpose if personalised and a contact with family just as a letter does. Most of all I wish all those close to me the same feeling on every other day of the year. I'll close on that – have got a feeling that I'm not alone with my thoughts and hope that you might share some, or all of them with me. John.

From the early days when the bike sales were on a continued upward curve many dealers opened a branch in a town perhaps some twenty miles away with two objectives. To grow the business and secondly to 'ring fence' the chance of a competitor encroaching. Standard business practice but years on I struggle to recall how many made a continued success of this. The dilemma was often caused by the encouraging franchise supplier who, though enjoying the performance of the original site with year on year sales, would identify the other 'open point' town and 'dangle the carrot'. What often happened is that the further investment in infrastructure and set up costs then coincided with a slowing of total market sales and the branch operation folded. Worse still it impacted on the original site. The solid small family company that had freehold premises and did everything that was asked of it and made profits year after year, succumbed to a form of greed thinly described as progression and empire building. Talking about progression it was around this time that on one of my car journeys I was tuned into a Lancashire radio interview.

The very successful owner of a local transport company was being asked as he approached retirement what he was going to do. The answer was not clear cut, apart from one loud and clear stated comment that he could not think about passing over to his sons and daughters his success as a gift of money 'as it would inhibit their natural progression in life.' First class reasoning. That struck home with me and going back in history to the idiot sons of the gentry's reference which does not apply to all of course, it could be the biggest disfavour you ever did for your loved ones. Not an easy one to ponder on for many now, as the £2,000 houses built and bought in the 1950's are being passed down to future generations for how much?

By this time my gathering book of quotes are becoming used as a life reference guide. I always had the inner feeling to resist a work promotion with suspicion as in 'Be Careful for what you Wish For' thinking of the book title used by Jeffrey Archer. A salary increase and thank you very much, but the hesitation when the opportunity came of a climb a few steps up the ladder to office based sales manager was difficult. I did not have the aptitude or interest perhaps to further my qualifications to a business degree to qualify for management. Or even more, the suggestion of a move to London or other business HQ. I felt my home moving days were well and truly over and must count up some time, the number of places I did call home. The day to day work I had done most of my life was having the trust of people and hopefully they felt the same about me. I made a decent living out of exactly that, but always to respect that the employer paid my salary. Answer was always the same if a tricky dealing situation arose. Tell the truth and find a way round it to keep each side happy if possible. Experience of life and attitudes became a similar pattern but I was noticing towards the end of full time work, the pressures to perform increasing with ever increasing health and safety provisions in the workplace.

Some quite dramatic European driven legislation specifications changes to machines. A creeping erosion of profit margins to assert power to the supplier and a trend towards solus franchise reward structures. All designed perhaps to take the owners name from above the door and move to a corporate image. Times they are a changing and like most of my age group, we meet up from time to time and have a 'good old days chat.'

We all seem to agree on one thing and that was, the responsibility we were given to make our sales and distribution policy viable and long lasting. Trust was a key word and the loyalty and extra mile that both sides went to make it work spoke for itself. Days that are probably gone forever.

These years were also very settled which was a new strange in a way feeling for me. Perhaps at last the long term efforts had worked of what I wanted to achieve in life?... and I had no reason to want for more. If only it was that simple-some perhaps are content to drift on, but I do try, it seems, to not recognise age as any barrier till inevitable common sense permeates through. As many times in life all you have to do is wait sometimes for destiny to take over and remember to enjoy what you have and not what you wish for. As I reached my 59th birthday in 2002 I had a talk with Massimo Mirosi. The same one who had stocked me up with Parmesan cheese at the earlier NEC show and both of us having been round a long time, realised that the market surge in steady increasing sales every year was at last slowing down. The same cycle that comes and goes and reminds us all to enjoy what we have when the going is good. Perhaps no need for the five sales reps that Piaggio now had out on the road he told me, plus a comment made that in Italy the age of sixty it was seen as the normal retirement for outside sales staff. Did I want to consider calling it a day and an arrangement could be made?

Sounded like a good idea to me and the idea was put on the back burner for a while and within 18 months a plan for me to take early retirement evolved. That's what happened and I had the pleasure of three months at home on gardening leave to adjust as the tomato growing season approached.

My retirement was short lived and the inevitable revisit in life to working again for my friend Giuseppe Tranchina (GT) and long standing appreciation society member like myself, of Sicilian TV's Inspector Montalbano. After leaving Piaggio he had returned to the UK to be appointed MD for another sporty Italian brand in Aprilia. They had recently closed their base in Stranraer in Scotland and moved to Stockport, only one hour's drive away from home in St Annes. Here we go again I thought. Talk about same face – different place. This time I was to be part time working 3 days a week and self employed as a sales agent and it was a perfect arrangement that lasted for some 6 years.

Chapter Thirteen

During these years a big feature was the planning we made for our leisure time and annual pilgrimage especially to Switzerland we first started in June 1989. Still the same Alpenrose Hotel, Wengen in the Berner Oberland as first choice and we never seem to tire of the location. On one particular late perfect afternoon, I sat with a pad and pen on a sun lounger in the garden and wrote the following short description of my day and the surroundings. That morning we had travelled to the viewing platform atop the Jungfrau Mountain reached by the most impressive train journey through a tunnel carved out in the mountainside a century ago. The views simply stunning. That day and my thoughts before dinner were of perfection. This short description I wrote then was to remember this day and in particular -the hotel and surroundings and when life is good to enjoy and reflect. I called it 'Ever been to Heaven'

EVER BEEN TO HEAVEN?
Sun loungers dotted between pollarded chestnut trees, on a daisy and grass bedecked terrace, subtly blend in

shades of green and white. It's a haven of peace and tranquillity with a view of the most stunning land-scape. Its mid-June at the Alpenrose Hotel in Wengen, Switzerland and the sun beats down from a cobalt sky. Alpine zephyrs carry a day long chorus of birdsong, with ever dominant blackbird leading the ensemble. A day earlier and stair rods of rain, sprinkled with hailstone, hammered onto the same terrace, throwing out tiny flints and spatters of earth from the cobbled surround.A pine scented air rises from the River Lutschine far below – its distant murmur carrying glacial melt and summer rain, onwards to the lakes of Brienz and Thun. Have you ever been to Heaven – or at least had a vision what it may be? Well – here's a chance of a preview for the many, mostly British, who have come to this alpine retreat of a hotel, year after year. It has been in the same family ownership for 125 years and perhaps, more important, it is family run with a pride and attention to detail. We "discovered" it in 1989 and have been back most years since, as early summer visitors, to walk and see the alpine flowers at their best. The cog railway from the Lauterbrunnen valley stops at Wengen (say it with a V) then carries on upwards, with its winter skiers and summer walkers. The grandeur of the year round snow clad vista of the Eiger and Jungfrau mountain ranges are a perfect back drop – a majestic carving that nature does best.

A few minutes fairly steep walk downhill from the rail station, leads to this quiet terrace and 'second home' for so many. Think hazy chocolate box scene, or even misty Scottish glens as portrayed by Landseer with tow-ering snow clad peaks and sloping alpine pastures. Think Swiss efficiency and attention to detail, with discreet and ever courteous friendly service. Take excellent, simple, wholesome food prepared in the most delicious manner as a formality. Imagine an elegant pine clad dining room with the finest engraved and chinging crystal glassware atop white starched table cloths. Remember only the still night hours, on down filled duvets, with occasional morning slumber broken by the clunk of a distant cowbell.

Experience the blazing sun and lashing rain of short violent summer storms that change the panorama as a daily slide show. Muse at a nigh on traffic free world – a whirr of electric cart and hoot of climbing train as the only reminders.

Remember as you walk, or perhaps doze the afternoon away, you are 4,000 feet above sea level. It's a fresher and cleaner world than the one we live in – of over populated town and city. Take all this as your insight to heaven perhaps? Your intimate interlude in a somehow unreal place, that's unchanged in a fast moving world outside. Many find a special place in their lives where they have been able to return to – a place to relax, to reminisce, to seek peace.

We found this. A very special thank you to the family von Allmen.

Alpenrose Hotel,
Wengen, Switzerland,
CH 3823
Tel: +41 033 855 3216
www.alpenrose.ch

-John Featherstone (June 2006)

These great times as a sixty plus to gently coast out of a full time working life gave me lots of insights into the changes of public attitudes and demands. The banter that the shop staff could have with the customer perhaps in years past, now replaced with a correctness of flicking through the under counter manual of "The Sale of Goods Act" and "Consumer Credit Law. Section 75". Mind blowing consumer over protection edicts to remember to prevent digging big holes for yourself and your business with internet advised law quoting customers.

I wish the staff of any business today in the trade that gave me such a fantastic living perseverance and hope that simple common sense law changes are made. The gentle letters of protest that I wrote to the motorcycle trade magazine some 30 years earlier as "confused and puzzled" of St Annes were attempts at workplace humour in a way to right a perceived wrong, or to laugh at others having first laughed at myself. The pleasure and enthusiast sharing has been ripped out of the whole process of bike sales. Not an overnight matter by any means and reflective of society today and as my working life draws to a close. I think of the dramatic changes in the last 10 years or so to erosion of working profit margins and the replacement with big stick bonus on achievement. Not drawing too much on the good old days for reference but humour seems to have gone on the back burner of life. Everything seems so complicated and phraseology to try and outdo. Are we are getting so tetchy perhaps the opportunity to rant through Facebook style media is so much easier – we can all be orators in the auditorium of cyber space but very rarely stand up and be counted when the opportunity arises.

Still keeping my collection of quotes for other usage, I did a bit of digging to find who actually coined the cracker of a line "assistant heads will have to roll for this" Result inconclusive, but used for lots of situations. Recently resurrected in 2012 for the demise of the short lived career of George Entwistle, appointed the Director General of the BBC for some 54 days culminating in a gigantic £240K annual salary pay off. Crisis – what crisis, as the press had a field day criticising the BBC establishment. Always the one subject that fills my working class roots thoughts of injustice with disbelief. Rewarded for failure like half the football managers in the game today? The archaic class system that perpetrates seemingly onward and upward to this day is bombproof. I was introduced to this ancient control system as an eleven year old at grammar school at the start of my story, knowing little of the hierarchy that controlled a school such as that. A life that has its ups and downs and protection usually through a family in the growing years or perhaps a union (or united) environment in the industrial work place that follows. Even a tidy white or blue collar bound career in whatever skills you possess protected by established and fair principles. The basics make common sense of standing and pulling together but often human nature takes its desire to spoil the party.

None of these can seemingly touch the ultimate top slice of society that is still alive and well and known today, as always, as the Old Boys network. The occasional 'outing' to show that reforms are under way, but the clandestine resentment of interference is a mantra. So that's what my 'famous quotes' hobby does for me-starts me off on a rant. But I don't watch Eastenders or Coronation Street, so I am untouched by the real world.

I owe the use of a simple quote always lurking in my mind to another Suzuki colleague Clare Hutley I worked with in the eighties. He quietly believed that luck does not exist in life and I will agree with that principle. Goes like this 'Luck is the place where planning and preparation meets opportunity' and attributed to Lucius Annaeus Seneca, a Roman senator and philosopher 4BC – 65AD. A further search comes up with an equally profound observation.

'True happiness is to enjoy the present without anxious dependence on the future. Not to amuse ourselves with either hopes or fears, but to rest satisfied with what we have-which is sufficient, for he that is so, wants for nothing. The greatest blessings of mankind are within our reach. A wise man is content with his lot whatever it may be, without wishing for what he has not.'

Back to normal living, out on the road calling back on motorcycle shops and thinking I have got to pack this lot in soon – but I still love the challenge so why stop? If the body says that's it Feathers-call it a day then that will apply. Or if I don't make the necessary sales targets then GT will say it for me. This time round the job is the same, but different. A large dealership in Stoke on Trent run by some great guys who had the ability not just to sell in the traditional area around them in the Midlands but by some clever advertising achieved it nationwide. They also had the magic asset of a hefty financial credit line to be able to buy more than anyone else and actively promote sales and sell UK wide. Very successful, but alas the smaller dealer who was buying just a few machines some 200 miles up the road felt threatened. And fast forward to the present market and the absolute revolution of internet buying and the intrusion of debatable restrictive Euro legislation into the UK culture. Probably all well researched sensible health and safety based technical advances and legal restrictive hoops to jump through to prevent us killing ourselves, but the perception of how to regulate our roads industry should be firmly based in the UK and not in Brussels. Our culture and attitude is different and integration of one application to cover all European countries ill founded.

Not a level playing field perhaps and another reason that the whole structure as in many trades is turned upside down. Big difference with the very technically advanced two wheels of today is that they do need to be fettled and looked after by skilled technicians as the enthusiast or commuter can no longer fiddle and fix. Quick conclusion and crystal ball for the future? A network of service centres and display machines and only one central UK depot called Amazon Bikes to supply every potential two wheel user. That's an ill researched forecast from confused and puzzled of St Annes who says he has retired fully from writing to trade magazines.

And I was also given the accounts in Northern Ireland and Dublin to go to which were an absolute pleasure, because I could hardly get a word in edgeways with that lot across the water. A flight from the local airport here in Blackpool with a tarmac stop in the Isle of Man to remember the many visits. Stunning views when the weather is clear and the approach in a small plane to Belfast Lough and the Titanic shipyards of Harland and Wolff. The Irish are never lost for a word or a solution to any situation that arises. Terrific off beat humour that's their speciality perhaps needed at times of working with all the troubled history. Meant an overnight stay once a month perhaps, but the hospitality and friendship from ex racers like Phil Mc Callen and Jeremy McWilliams in Belfast and all their staff was welcoming. The train ride up to Coleraine to see Wilfie Conner and family who was always ready for the updates on life around the trade.

It also took me back to Donegall Pass in the city centre to keep a friendship started some 30 years earlier with James Mc Donnell who ran the original Vespa dealership there. Always the entertaining stories to tell, or yarns as he called them -which apparently Rudyard Kipling said is the way history should have been taught, so we could remember it easier. Jim Mc Donnell was the one who related the phrase 'Get On' when he described to me that those words were the typical street talk enquiry for a young Belfast lad coming into the shop wanting to buy a scooter. Just short and direct. Door opens-young man points to a bike on display and says: 'How do ah get on?' I told the story in passing to Steve Kenward now MCI chief and it's now used for sales promotions in the industry.

Chapter Fourteen

Time now to let my working days go quietly away, as a new school of learning and trauma comes into the lives of Mr and Mrs J. Featherstone. Ballroom Sequence Dancing!

To start at the beginning of my introduction to dance that goes back to teenage days. Ballroom dancing would have taken me to my first visit to the Winter Gardens with mates from school who I survived boating holidays with on the Norfolk Broads. No correction-Mum and sister Shirley would have made a valiant attempt to show me the steps of the valeta dance as a disinterested 12 year old perhaps. Couple this with the first introduction to licensed premises around 1960, the arrival on the music scene of Chubby Checker and the Twist and most important the chance to 'cop' for girls. Pulling the birds was a later expression.

What better opportunity than to be living in Blackpool and the home of dancing at the Tower Ballroom and the Winter Gardens complex nearby. Victor Sylvester, later a famous bandleader but in 1922 he won the first ever ballroom dance championship competition here with his partner Phyllis Clarke and Blackpool to this day will always be the home of ballroom dance. The days of graceful waltz dance moves, orchestral music and a tribute to centuries of tradition of dress and social grace. Manners and protocol of dance traditions to allow the sexes to meet in an approved and proper way as the text books might record.

A far cry from what we had in mind, as the awakening late fifties and early sixties arrived to present a group of girls standing around in a circle with handbags on the packed floor of the Winter Gardens, pretending that the last thing they wanted was for a boy to ask them to dance. When I say 'ask them to dance' we would not really have a clue of any formal asking, chat up line or even what to do as dance steps if they magically agreed.

With knotted stomach and head down I could perhaps have leaned over to one in the group and mumbled 'Do you want to do this one with me' as the resident band attempted the latest Bill Haley rock and roll number or the awakening lyrics and music from Elvis Presley. These often fruitless visits to satisfy newly awakened lust. Other attempts to attract girls were made when Bill Taylor or Phil Crossley were able to borrow their parents car and we went to village halls such as Winmarleigh or St Michaels on a Saturday night in the Fylde coast area around Blackpool. With an often strike rate of zero in "crumpet conquest" we convinced ourselves perhaps that we were acting like real men in standing around and getting noticed. This was a short lived phase and I never mastered any dance routine from jive to waltz or quickstep. Years went by in life and motorbikes and snooker took the place of dance interest.

Many years later Jan and I did go to dance classes started in Blackpool by Ken and Pat Rayner at their Melody Ballroom near Talbot Road. Great teachers and when they retired, a from time to time attendance at classes over the years run by the local council in school halls. Whatever steps or routines we learned faded from the memory bank and it was always going to be 'we should start dancing lessons again'. It took many years for us to finally take up a suggestion by lifelong friends Ken and Alice Croft to think about going to ballroom sequence dances.

This would have been in 2005 and one afternoon we went with them to St. Christopher's Church hall on Hawes Side Lane, which just happens to be right next door to the Hawes Side Junior School where I was practising plagiarism as a schoolboy some fifty years earlier writing copied adventure stories.

Sequence is a predetermined set of dance moves to sixteen bars of music. Usually referred to as an inventive dance that allows the couples on the floor to start the waltz, quickstep or Latin moves all at the same time to a different music tempo. Object is that the same steps of each dance are taken by each couple in an anti clockwise formation pattern with flowing moves at the same time. Quite simply the same designed steps as in freestyle dance, but the group and social aspect becomes the attraction for many.

That afternoon was the start of a whole new chapter in our lives that carries on to this day. We went in with Alice and Ken to the recently modernised dance floored church hall and were immediately made welcome by the dance teachers David and Rita Harrod who live locally in Bispham. There were around 25 or so couples in the room with chairs circled round the sides for seating between dances and clearly everyone knew each other. All similar ages to ourselves in the main, with several ladies who danced together and no shortage of conversation before the dance session got under way. The first sequence dance we ever saw was the Mayfair Quickstep and as they always do, David and Rita led off for the first few bars of the CD music he plays to suit each dance. What an eye opener for us as we sat there and watched as every other couple in the room got up and danced the same steps. Obviously some found it easier and were lighter on their feet, but these couples had probably all been dancing for many years. Noticeable straight away and very relaxed and a delight to watch were mother and daughter Stella and Elizabeth Jones. Not that we knew any others by name at the time, but we were asked by many if we had danced before. So that was the first dance and followed by a waltz and a rumba and a saunter and they all kept getting up from their seats and dancing each dance. How could they possibly remember all the steps and in the sequence order and age certainly not a barrier?

Tea break came after the first hour as we sat quite amazed and were joined by Rita, who was interested to know what if any dance experience we had. The reply did not take long and interestingly she said that she and David would be starting a beginner's class in the near future. Would we be interested?

And that's how it all started. I mean by that, the dance teaching of steps and shall we say stress in our lives that had been absent for many years. Controlled in the main minor altercations and disputes over procedural progress or lack of on the dance floor, as Jan and I took on a new life project. We entered into this new learning curve with enthusiasm and consideration for each other's ability. Well I think we did and after many years together certainly know how to behave in public especially and have never have had a serious difference of opinion for ages-he said with some lack of conviction.

Within weeks we had started our new beginner's class at St Marks Church hall in Layton on a Saturday. Just a few couples like ourselves either new to sequence dance or lapsed ballroom dancers from earlier years. Enthusiasm was there and in the main we were quite pleased after the first hour's small group instruction on the basic steps of the Mayfair Quickstep and then in following weeks step by step teaching of the Rumba One and the Catherine Waltz. All good standard and well known inventive dances popular to this day. We tried to keep calm, pay attention and learn. At first one or two terse words spoken in private when clearly we both forgot which steps came next –then sadly panic mode and words said that bubbled into a public display of lack of confidence, annoyance and barely controlled seething rage at times.

Always full of respect for each other's feelings to start each lesson, we gingerly progressed into the first sequence of steps that we had both forgotten from the last week's class – but just guessed what they were.

I would then hear the following less than helpful remark. 'You are doing it wrong' Jan said in what I considered to be a louder voice than necessary. Followed by the quieter mutter back from me through thin lips 'No-you are supposed to step back Jan.' Within seconds my gentle and firm clasped hand hold has turned into a vice like grip without me realising apparently (well, that's what I was told later). She says: 'will you stop pushing me'. It is 'she' by now because I do not wish to refer to her as Jan any more.

Soothing orchestral background CD music for the other dancers of 'Fly me to the Moon' goes pleasantly on, as another understanding couple behind carefully sweep past pretending they are deaf. 'I can't take anymore of this' is said by my dance partner (she) as we make another stumble forward with blanked minds... but help is at hand! As it has been for hundreds of willing and distraught souls over the years of learning classes, as the calming presence of David and Rita instantly appear alongside and split us up. Wonderful expression that – they split us up to then restore peace in our time!

Experience told them that once again timing is essential to repair an imminent breakdown in relationships and they carry just the right know how and calming presence to make it work. Peace is restored in seconds, as I am firmly taken in hand with: 'Put your hands on my shoulders-and do it with me' from Rita and then I am sturdily guided and talked through the remaining bars of the dance steps in a daze of relief. If only I could have seen what happened to 'she' I would have witnessed the same treatment, with Jan being guided effortlessly around the room by dance teacher and experienced mind reader David Harrod.

Matters then improved dramatically as we both decided this was a wonderful sharing of time together with a satisfying feeling when we did manage to learn a dance to a comfortable standard. We asked to take private lessons with them in addition to our weekly group classes and this was something we looked forward to every Wednesday for several weeks, to have that vital one to one guidance. Not just the correct steps but posture and dance hold, don't look down at your feet, remember to breathe, shoulders back, don't saw your arms up and down... these are my words not the correct descriptive terms they used!

But within a few short lessons our confidence and relaxed attitude improved. We even nearly stopped squabbling over whose fault it was when a mistake was made-correction I gave up arguing and probably said 'sorry, that was me going wrong there my love.' Diplomacy being the better part of valour.

In 2005 we had found a new way to enjoy learning the old and the new inventive dances that are part of this excellent social pastime for many. A decade later and we still enjoy our twice weekly visits to David and Rita's always well attended dance sessions. Mostly fifty year old plus regulars and many who have literally been dancing all their lives in summer and winter. Always the same consensus of opinion that not only does it exercise the body but more importantly keeps the grey cells from going into standby. The Fylde Coast and Blackpool being the home of ballroom dance, also has the distinction of having probably the longest surviving dance club in the UK in the Holy Trinity Church hall in Dean Street in the town. A tribute to the committee and members who have kept the doors open every Friday night for dancing and recently celebrated their 80th year.

Another pleasure over the years has being involved with organising some dance holidays with our group and in particular two excellent trips to a pleasantly warm and sunny Cyprus in March to the Athena Beach hotel in Paphos. My only regret is that this excellent way to share life together is only really taken up by the older generation dancers and so often it is the man who is reluctant to go along to learn in the first place. Perhaps that macho reserve?

Strange thing is that many of us remark on, is that once we are hooked it is often the bloke who had to be dragged there in the first place, who becomes the prime mover and insists on going to as many dances as possible! Not least it is also a wonderful opportunity for ladies to dance together and has always been a long established tradition to hopefully continue for years to come.

My reference to sequence dancing would not be complete without the mention of an exceptional and intuitive teacher of dance that we have in David Harrod. A gifted man whose ability to not just relate the steps of the new inventive dance by leading off and explanation, it is that special reaching out to what seems to be just for you to succeed, that brings his lessons to life. Seeming unceasing energy and personality, that encourages you to "just try once more for me" as he often implores. Couple that with an encouraging double act humour and we all know why sequence dance is alive and well on the Fylde Coast.

There is a downside to me writing this reference to him if he does indeed choose to read it, or it is brought to his attention. He will dismiss it, saying he is just doing his job. Well, he can think what he likes!-I will go with the majority opinion of fellow dancers, who know they have had an extended and pleasure filled social life, based for years on the weekly venues and dance holidays that David and Rita organise.

Chapter Fifteen

After the private lessons all those years ago and the continuing Saturday beginners class we felt more confident and started to go the the regular weekly venues. If not to venture on to the floor with the wide array of dances at least to watch and enjoy and most of all learn. Very pleasant and new friends made. A foursome in particular we met every week and took to sitting with at St Christopher's Church hall every Monday afternoon. This is where a particular conversation has a twist and thought provoking memory that, not for the first time I chose to write down for use later. I called it a 'walk without talk' and the description fits.

A WALK WITHOUT TALK
In April 1998 I fulfilled an ambition and retraced the steps of Alfred Wainwright and did (like many others before me), the Coast to Coast walk from St Bees in Cumbria to Robin Hood's Bay in Yorkshire.

Fourteen years later and approaching sixty nine, I can look back and think with some pride that I was able to achieve the 192 miles in the suggested 12 days, with pack on back and for the main part staying in quite good bed and breakfast accommodation.

So that really should be it... but not quite.

Some two years ago my daughter Judith suggested that her and I might retrace part of the walk. A grand idea of a bit of father and daughter bonding. It worked well -I chose days two and three of AW's suggested route starting at Ennerdale through the very scenic Honister Pass and overnight in Rosthwaite, Borrowdale at an excellent hotel. The next day we completed a further section to arrive and be met at Grasmere... only difference from the first time was the extra miles that must have been added!! Especially the longer than remembered slog over Greenup Edge and out of the Ennerdale Valley towards the mine workings at the top of Honister. Twenty odd years younger than me, she fared little better with blisters and leg pain-but worth every bit of it.

So over these fourteen years it has come into conversation from time to time that I "did the C to C". A confession that I might have even mentioned first to others who may, or may not, have been interested. Not quite the marathons of today or even swimming the channel, or climbing Everest.

None the less it always lurked in the mind as my little bit of outdoor achievement, so I settled for a reply such as 'Oh – did you.? That must have been some walk then' as a compliment rather than the: 'You must have been mad' from the rather more direct. Whatever – it was and still is my tiny claim to fame.

Well it was, up till a few weeks ago, when I found something out that brought this memory to a retrospective sense of reality that makes it pale into total insignificance. Especially the times that I reflected upon in the years after doing the walk and actually enjoying a compliment here and there...indulgent wallowing perhaps?

In the last few years my wife Jan and I have become interested in Sequence Dancing. A wonderful activity I could recommend to others, especially a retirement keep fit and social thing, that keeps body and mind in trim. At our local church hall I met a man I will call Tom (which was my Dad's name and seems just right for the story I have to tell) and we tend to sit with him and his wife and their friends most weeks.

He is some years older than me-an amazing active ninety one in fact. Very quietly spoken with a dry sense of humour and as often happens topics like holidays, difficulty of learning of new dances, weather and all the usual day to day conversations take place. All good friendly banter and social meet ups.

Other than that I know little about him except that it was mentioned by others that he was a flight engineer flying Lancaster Bombers in World War 2.This is a man who in the past couple of years has shown a stoic resistance to an illness he is battling against and yet holidays and weekly dance sessions are a must for him, just as the smartness of appearance is paramount.

I don't have an extensive knowledge of WW2 history but was aware that as the final months of the war drew to a close, many of the POW's in the Stalag Luft camps were forced to march away from the east of Germany presumably as the Russians advanced, in the depths of winter with little or no adequate food or clothing. A few minutes internet research tells of the horrors of these...and many died on the way. In recent weeks there have been some excellent TV documentary pro-grammes shown including Bomber Boys and the whole dreadful period was brought back of the early 1940's – I'm not even two years old at the time but this is not distant history.

Still no admission from Tom that he was even there. It was left to a friend of his to confirm that he was indeed one of the Bomber Boys – shot down in 1944 and interned in Stalag Luft 7 where one of the most infamous and gruelling 150 mile walks was made in January 1945.

I asked him one day if indeed he minded that I men-tioned it. 'Not at all' was the reply and he told me the story of events in a matter of fact way, later producing his internment papers with Nazi insignia and ID tag he has kept-just as you would if you showed around a birth certificate. Quite humbling and so typical of this quiet man.

It did not take me long after that afternoon to look again at the diary notes I had kept for my walk of choice some fourteen years earlier.

They have gone back in a drawer for now and if the subject of the Coast to Coast ever crops up, I might mention that I know a man who never needed to talk ...
                                    -*John Featherstone (March 2012)*

There is a man I know who does know how to talk even more than me and his name is Richard – or Rick to everyone else except his mother Jan who refuses to call her eldest son that name. I mentioned his name earlier in my story when he went with us to Canada to see friends and he was able to enjoy watching the Toronto Maple Leafs world famous ice hockey team play.

Quite special for him as he was a regular with the Blackpool Seagulls ice hockey team in the seventies. To this day he still has involvement with the same original team members of yesteryear and is active at the local rink when his well past it body is put back on the ice to perform. Reckons he can show the youngsters of today his moves and tricks-at least for a few minutes before he is carried off to rest.

More importantly he is the one I turn to for help and have done for years. I do not need to wire a three pin plug these days, but if I struggle to knock a nail in straight, then he is there to help. Blown out garden fence panels to replace, computer set ups and IT information but most of all a good trusted reliable friend as well. I declined his kind offer to show me how to use Sat Nav. Thanks Richard and keep coming as long as you want for tea every week and giving me a rest from telling stories.

I was asked what inspiration I got from writing short life stories over the years. I know where the impetus came from and that was my Nan at an early age with her story telling. May have been a well embellished story, but it was probably based on a true experience and carried a message for future life. Then reading a whole genre of classic books available to me and later the never forgotten encouragement of Jack Benson and others to put my feeling and expression onto paper.

I never really understood much of correct grammatical expressions and usage, but again relied on the old belief that if it sounds right to you when you read it back and makes sense-then settle for that. Write from the heart and experience of the confidence of truth you believe in. Rudyard Kipling is often quoted for the beautiful thought provoking prose of IF he penned in 1895...or most likely remembered as "one day you will be a man my son"

I also find the inspiration as many will in certain song lyrics which is an easier form of poetry to remember. In 1969 Malcolm Roberts had a top ten hit with 'Love is all I have to Give.' Sometimes it's just one line and evocative music that lifts you to make it personal. Some might say we all practice plagiarism and it is the best tribute to be inspired by a word or line that you can then take to your own interpretation.

Last year 2015 was quite memorable in many ways for quite a few ups, but some downs as well. Having finally, finally stopped working in the motorcycle industry even part time I was penning more short stories of life when one day the phone rang and Philip Youles from Blackburn called me. We had kept contact for many years after he took on the Piaggio scooter franchise and with wife Louise had expanded his business to a branch in Manchester and today is a leading dealer in the UK for Triumph motorcycles as well.

Upshot of the call was that with Martin Marshall from Aberdeen (another colleague and friend of mine from past selling days) they had decided to recruit me for a liaison role to improve membership of the NMDA. That is the National Motorcycle Dealers Association of which they are both committee members. True to form I was not being asked, but told that they wanted me to do a series of visits to northern area shops to remind the trade of the advantages of membership. Reason for selection, without interview or CV, was that I knew a lot of the dealer principals and that I would possibly be let in the door in the first place to state a case. A six month deal was worked out and I reasoned that if my first job was as a paper boy at thirteen earning twelve shillings and sixpence a week, I could at least feel I was still working some sixty years on – but this time having to pay tax. Had a great six months doing the rounds but the extra mileage was taking its toll, but I enjoyed it none the less and got some results. A chance to meet up again with a very supportive and association manager in Steve Latham who I report in to. The regular travelling is finished now, but I am still in contact for NMDA stand attendance at the annual Expo trade show for some three days run by British Dealer News in January every year at Stoneleigh.

Those were the ups, but the downs came with some holiday re visits that made us think that nothing perhaps does stay the same. Over the years if we found a particular haven like the Alpenrose hotel in Switzerland or a lovely B & B in Grasmere or the Cotswolds we tended to return to and enjoy them in the following years. More recently we find that times they are indeed a changing or it is perhaps us seeing a standard we took for granted being eroded? Nothing too important of course but always need to fall back on humour to rescue the moment if we start to think what are we doing here? If you sat down for dinner in a restaurant the question might be 'Good evening sir/madam. Are you ready to order, or do you want me to come back in a little while. Can I get you a drink in the meantime?' Pretty standard sort of introduction and very acceptable, though the sir and madam reference a bit dated perhaps but still nice. Not sure about the today's approach of: 'Now then – what can I get you guys'.

Time for waiter to be beckoned by her indoors who might say perhaps: 'Now then young man. First of all – we are not you guys'. But we have tired now of any attempted correction process and tend to be selective in what we do and where we go. Don't get angry –get even. Or something like that as we sit in a picnic area eating our butties and drinking the flask of coffee we made, just as we like it.

More importantly and on a serious note we were making regular visits to see a very poorly sister at her home in Skipton Yorkshire.

In early May I had a phone call from friends Graham and Sue Best of Kegra in Southend with the sad news that Valerie Hamilton from Newcastle had died. Paul and Val of Motech Scooters have many happy memories to share with me from them taking over Angelo's Scooter repair shop and building it into the North East's number one dealership for Piaggio Vespa. On the 21st May I set off from home early to by car travel to the North East to attend her funeral and this day proved to be another of those times when people and places takes you towards an eventful decision – and not for the first time in my life. I reached the market town of Kirkby Stephen and just by chance saw again the sign for the Jolly Farmers Guest House on the main street. I called in and met Carol Pepper who I had last seen in April 1998 when I stopped there overnight on my Coast to Coast walk. I admitted to being not the most regular of guest visitors and said I had called in by chance as memories took me back all those years. Had a chat about all the guests still doing the C to C she has had over the years and I mentioned that I remembered well the rainy slog over Nine Standards to Keld the next day after leaving Kirkby Stephen.

She picked up a paperback in the lounge: 'Have you seen this book by Amanda Owen?' 'No what's that about' I replied. Handing it to me for a look, I read the cover title 'The Yorkshire Shepherdess'-how I left city life behind to raise a family and a flock by Amanda Owen. Carol suggested it was an excellent read and would be the farm I walked past called Ravenseat as I trudged into Keld village some seventeen year earlier. I read the book and it is a fantastic story of her life and what to do, other than some aimless wandering. Most of all she tells it as it is with matter of fact honesty and simplicity.

I continued on my journey but my mind was in 'think back' mode the rest of that sad day as I went on to South Shields and said farewell to Val. It made me think of the regular visits Jan and I were making to see a sister slipping away from life, but as ever always asking about others. Within weeks we had a day trip out to Ravenseat Farm and met with Clive and Amanda Owen and had the most delicious scones and tea served by eldest daughter Raven.

Once again in life I was on a revisit to memories past and the quirkiness of names and places from my early days and that we were sitting on a picnic bench yards from the Whitsundale Beck I had waded through eighteen years ago. Amanda's father, a knowledgeable motorcycle repairer, used to regularly visit Earnshaws Motorcycles in Huddersfield who sold Suzuki motorcycles. The same shop I called every few weeks on working for Suzuki GB in the seventies as the sales rep and possibly met him. How many more prompts did I need to 'get on with it lad' as Jack Benson told me. So that was it.

Out came the old files and handwritten notes from way back. On a recent cruise holiday I spent many an hour on a pitching deck in the Bay of Biscay writing in a notebook. Memories of dates and places and seeing again in my mind the fifties and sixties and recalling stories and visions to remember when back home. It must have worked because just as I struggle now to remember what happened last week, those prompt lines I wrote down would easily bring a childhood or teens memory back to vivid life. I was able to live it all through again and see the faces of yesteryear. What was the best ever job you had, could be asked of me with a special memory to go with it? No need to think too long on that.

As a carefree teenager driving an open topped Land Rover early on a sunny August Bank holiday morning from Central Beach, Blackpool on to the miles of tide uncovered sand. In between I would have been combing my hair in what I thought was a Tony Curtis lookalike style and naturally wearing sun glasses for maximum bird pulling effect. I was delivering ice cream containers into the vans placed on pitches ready for the holiday hordes to descend and buy the cornets and wafers. Speed limit around 5 mph near the promenade access slades that led down onto the sand carefully wending through already placed deckchairs and children digging holes. But then up and away through the gears racing under the North Pier stanchions through sprayed pools of water and to the open spaces and hard packed beach sand banks of North Shore …foot down and happy with not a care in the world!!

The saddest day arrived on the 17th November and we went to Skipton to say goodbye.

That sister of mine was always writing poetry and bringing evocative words to life in cards and letters over the years. It was something I never really thought of doing, so here it is Shirley – my belated attempt at words for the last school I plan to attend.

THE SCHOOL OF LIFE

Keep your thoughts to yourself, if you think it is wiser
Or make your views known, if you seek a decider
Choice is for all – not just those on a throne
Listen to others and don't stand alone.

Freedom and respect are values to treasure
Take them to heart and make them your measure
Listen, then speak, words chosen with care
There's no winning or losing – so think what is fair.

Love is emotion – it's free and is given
No strings or conditions, so there's no price to pay
Feel sadness for those who take and do nothing
And can never enjoy the warmth of response.

Life is like love, a school room of learning
Both are exams of achieving and sharing
Many are praised for passing the tests
But only you know if you tried your best.

                    -John Featherstone (December 2015)

Reckon I have had a fortunate, not lucky experience of life and plan to continue to enjoy everything that comes my way, especially if it brings a smile with it. Blessed now with an enthusiastic nature to try and keep that smile, rather than having the earlier frown of youth. A thank you in advance to those I have yet to meet, who may one day reach out and take my hand if needed.

I will end on this one.

'There will come a time in every young man's life, when he comes to realise he knows as little as he thinks his father knows now.' I wish the next generation well, as they might have to push more treacle uphill than I did. If you manage to do it from time to time-enjoy the satisfaction.

'Well, I would say that wouldn't I.'

-John Featherstone (February 2016)

The Later Years...

Richard & John
with Mum.

With my two best
friends.

Ever the best
of friends.

Doing what we do best.

Secretary outside
the office.

My office in Summer.

David & Rita Harrod.

With Jude at
Heron's Reach.

Shirley with Jude & Amy.

Neil, Jude & Jan in Bluebell
Woods at Brock Bottom.

With Jan.

Lightning Source UK Ltd.
Milton Keynes UK
UKOW07f0120130416

272145UK00008B/30/P